D1542978

STAFF ONE: A PERSPECTIVE ON EFFECTIVE POLICE MANAGEMENT

EDWARD M. DAVIS

PRENTICE-HALL, INC., ENGLEWOOD CLIFFS, N.J. 07632

Library of Congress in Publication Data

DAVIS, EDWARD M., 1916-
   Staff one.

   Includes index.
   1. Police administration.   I. Title.
   HV7935.D38   363.2   78-1308
   ISBN 0-13-840256-6
   ISBN 0-13-840249-3 pbk.

Printed in the United States of America

10 9 8 7 6 5 4 3 2 1

PRENTICE-HALL, INTERNATIONAL, INC., *London*
PRENTICE-HALL OF AUSTRALIA PTY. LIMITED, *Sydney*
PRENTICE-HALL OF CANADA, LTD., *Toronto*
PRENTICE-HALL OF INDIA PRIVATE LIMITED, *New Delhi*
PRENTICE-HALL OF JAPAN, INC., *Tokyo*
PRENTICE-HALL OF SOUTHEAST ASIA PTE. LTD., *Singapore*
WHITEHALL BOOKS LIMITED, *Wellington, New Zealand*

17
\

Acknowledgments

A book by a first-time author must go through a special process. There are many mistakes that need to be made. You spin your wheels unnecessarily, but it all comes out all right in the end. With the right people, it can be easier. My daughter Mary Ellen endured these passages in their primitive stage as she taped my lectures at Chaminade College where these words germinated. Mrs. Helen Plischke and Miss Betty Lou Mabrie gave me letter-perfect copy to work with at every stage. And, two young lieutenants, Robert Taylor and David Brath, gave their evenings away from their families to assemble these pages into a comprehensible shape. I am deeply indebted to them for their help and friendship.

TO VIRGINIA

who has been the "rock" to which I have cleaved

Contents

Contents

Contents

Introduction

This is not a typical text on the subject of management. There are no definitions of POSCORB (planning, organizing, staffing, coordination, reporting, and budgeting), nor is there a lengthy comment on or a magical formula for the deployment of human resources. This is simply a guide to the management and supervision of people by a man who has been both a manager and a chief executive.

For years, books have been written on the subjects of management, attempting to explain the task of dealing with the complex problems generally associated with running an organization. In this book, I have attempted to explain not only some of the "how-to's," but, more important, the "why's."

It has been my observation that when a person understands the soul of his purpose, the "how-to" becomes much easier to comprehend. It is important that people be given some understanding of the philosophy behind their profession and the manner in which their boss operates. It is as if they were using the boss as a case study on management so that some day, when they themselves become managers, they may do the job better—or at least, as well.

This book has its setting in my police world, but there are several comments on leadership and executive peace that might be applied to other vocations within the private and public sectors. Although I am a policeman, I've made it a point to study things outside my specialty as well. I will, however, begin this text with a description of the basis for the policing function and its purpose.

Sir Robert Peel, the English statesman and founder of the British police system, expressed the idea that the ultimate measure of police effectiveness is the absence of crime and disorder. When policing organizations of the past noted an increase in crime, the single solution to that increase was a request for more resources. Today's administrator does not have the luxury of a bottomless well from which to draw budgetary resources. The ultimate provider of those resources, the taxpayer, has been drained. So people must be provided with police services that are furnished from fewer available dollars but that are not less effective. Additionally, the entire system responsible for such services must be made to provide them effectively and efficiently. Within the criminal justice field, this means that the police, the prosecutors, the courts, the correctional elements, and the legislatures must work together. Then, those elements and the people they serve must work together for the sake of society as a whole. This book describes how that might be accomplished.

As I achieved a position of influence in the Los Angeles Police Department and ultimately became its chief, I set out to take my organization across what I called the *Five Frontiers.* They were like uncharted seas; if the American police service was to succeed, it would be necessary to face and conquer those frontiers. Some, like bringing the people and the police together, or the police together with themselves, might be easy enough. Bringing the people together with other people to fight crime, or the police together with the rest of the criminal justice system so that they might work in concert, would be another story. Nevertheless, that was my course.

In many ways, large and small, I have seen great success. The key to that success, when the story of my tenure is written, will have been a curious combination of leadership traits and cooperation. In a very great sense, that is what this book is all about. We ask our leaders to lead us. We ask them to get us through the tough spots without too much harm and to keep us in the good times without meddling too much in our lives. That asks a great deal of our leaders. They are, after all, people of talent whose view of themselves is at all times quite favorable. It is important, therefore, that we ask what makes our leaders tick—that we suggest, as I have attempted to, some of the things that we should look for in the men we ask to lead us, and some of the human characteristics an ambitious future leader ought to cultivate. Quite naturally, the topics discussed here are things I try to practice myself. (Remember, I said that leaders frequently view their own perceptions with great favor.)

In quite another sense, there are factors having to do with leadership that are not personal factors. They involve organizational and social dynamics. Success in directing these forces to good purpose and, equally important, in keeping those forces from destroying good men and organizations comes under the heading of what I call maintaining "executive peace." It is a much-discussed subject in these days of tension and stress, and deservedly so. The crisis-torn world of policing our cities should be the subject of more attention than it has received. I am not pointing out the need for more political studies; we have seen enough of those. I am proposing a change in the criminal justice system so that it might be more responsive to the needs of the people we are supposed to be protecting. That is the best kind of peace for all of us.

How I achieved my own peace—while it is not complete,

I assure you—comes from a combination of recognition of the needs of those around me and a tenacious desire (some say malicious) to remind people who work for me how important they really are to the success of our organization. Oddly, there are many in an organization who believe that the boss is infallible, and that all they have to do is keep reminding him of that. Once you prove to those people how little you do know and how much you need them to make great strides, you and they will both achieve a much-needed peace of mind. (It helps if the boss can successfully accomplish his part of the job.)

There are some secrets to achieving that peace that I feel compelled to share with the reader. They are not shortcuts. They are devices for recognizing what makes the leader and his organization work smoothly and effectively.

That compulsion leads me to close with a short comment on organizational policies and philosophy for the police service. In my own organization, we have developed 20 "management principles" that we believe are critical to the provision of police service to the people. No organization, especially a police organization, can function without a clear view of what they are about. The principles offered here bring reality to the importance of shared thoughts and sound guidelines.

One of the closing chapters of this book describes various characteristics of most leaders, indicating that the effectiveness of a leader is best determined by what he leaves behind for others. I hope that I have ignited a spark for potential managers of the future and rekindled a flame for those who are already in the arena. Hopefully, this will make their fight a little easier.

I
POLICE WORK TODAY

By 1263, London had replaced compulsory service with a "standing watch" system. The watchmen carried a lantern and staff; some even carried a bell to warn others of their approach. These watchmen were supervised by a constable and were paid by the city. They were responsible for protecting property against fire, guarding the gates, and arresting those who committed crimes between sunset and daybreak.

Sir Robert Peel

As England entered the era of the Industrial Revolution, thousands of people began flocking to the towns. And as the towns grew, so did the problem of crime and disorder. Government and citizens alike demanded better protection. Each justice of the peace, within the newly created police offices, was authorized to hire six paid constables. By 1800, nine police offices were established within the metropolitan area of London. There was a regular night watch, special police to guard docks, markets, and so on, and also the "Bow Street Runners," who served notices and warrants for the courts. Yet crime continued to be a major problem.

Between 1822 and 1829, Sir Robert Peel, who was England's home secretary and was later to become prime minister, debated in Parliament on behalf of specific police reforms. His position was difficult, because it attempted to reconcile the idea of personal freedom with the necessity for the security of persons and property. Peel contended that while the police could not eliminate crime, the poor quality of selection and training contributed to social disorder. But some Englishmen thought that it was better to suffer from an occasional riot or theft than to give a group of officers the power to remove personal liberty and to demand that a person face a court trial.

The debate temporarily resolved the issue of whether the police were needed to maintain order and protect society from criminal encroachment; and in 1829, Peel's Metropolitan

Police Act was passed and he founded the London police force. (Its members have ever since been known as "peelers" or "bobbies.")

The life story of Sir Robert Peel had a profound effect on me as I grew in my profession, and his ideas became dominant factors in my own thinking about life and government. There is something basically civilized about much of the British way of life, and that certainly applies to Peel's approach to the relationship between the citizenry and its police. From him and his disciples have come basic tenets that are fundamental, even now. In my agency, they have been enhanced by my own thinking, primarily to make them more contemporary.

Here are the principles, evolved from Peel's philosophy, that still guide the English police today:

1. To prevent crime and disorder, as an alternative to their repression by military force, and by severity of legal punishment.

2. To recognize always that the power of the police to fulfill their functions and duties is dependent on public approval of their existence, actions, and behaviour, and on their ability to secure and maintain public respect.

3. To recognize always that to secure and maintain the respect and approval of the public means also the securing of the willing co-operation of the public in the task of securing observance of laws.

4. To recognize always that the extent to which the cooperation of the public can be secured diminishes, proportionately, the necessity of the use of physical force and compulsion for achieving police objectives.

5. To seek and to preserve public favour, not by pandering to public opinion, but by constantly demonstrating absolutely impartial service to Law, in complete independence of policy, and without regard to the justice or injustice of the substance of individual laws; by ready offering of individual service and friendship to all members of the public without regard to their wealth or social

standing; by ready exercise of courtesy and friendly good-humour; and by ready offering of individual sacrifice in protecting and preserving life.

6. To use physical force only when the exercise of persuasion, advice and warning is found to be insufficient to obtain public co-operation to an extent necessary to secure observance of law or to restore order; and to use only the minimum degree of physical force which is necessary on any particular occasion for achieving a police objective.

7. To maintain at all times a relationship with the public that gives reality to the historic tradition that the police are the public and that the public are the police; the police being only members of the public who are paid to give full-time attention to duties which are incumbent on every citizen, in the interests of community welfare and existence.

8. To recognize always the need for strict adherence to police-executive functions, and to refrain from even seeming to usurp the powers of the judiciary of avenging individuals or the State, and of authoritatively judging guilt and punishing the guilty.

9. To recognize always that the test of police efficiency is the absence of crime and disorder, and not the visible evidence of police action in dealing with them.[1]

Current Status

What should be kept in mind here is that throughout English history, whenever the government or the rulers have found it necessary to utilize military force to subjugate their own people, they have been unsuccessful. Perhaps the most recent example is that in Northern Ireland. Instead of having local police officers handle that situation, British troops have been used to bring about a forced peace. The relationship between the people of Northern Ireland and their government is obviously not a very good one.

[1]Charles Reith, *A Short History of the British Police* (New York: Oxford University Press, 1948), pp. 64–65. By permission of the Oxford University Press.

For years, all governments, not just that of England, have been using similar methods to bring about civil peace. Sometimes force is necessary, but when it is used by a government against its own countrymen, it does not necessarily result in a satisfactory resolution of civil problems. Peel recognized that nearly 150 years ago in his principles.

In most nations where the police force was not developed and conceived through an actual design, as it was in England, it has not been very effective. Perhaps the primary distinction lies in the deep sense of purpose of the British police, and a knowledge of who they are and from where their power comes. Most English police officers are very sensitive and feel an identification with their community.

THE AMERICAN EXPERIENCE

In America, the development of the policing system was much different from that of the English model. The colonists brought with them to this country the watch and ward system, a structure of law enforcement that was familiar to them from their homeland. Many colonies adopted the British constabulary night-watch system. The night watchmen would walk the streets checking for fires and giving a cry that all was well. The mutual-pledge system of England was used, constables were appointed by the Crown's governor for towns, and major landowners were appointed as sheriffs for the county. After the American Revolution and the birth of democracy, sheriffs tended to be elected by a vote of the people, and constables were often appointed by elected public officials.

As America began growing and expanding, crime and civil disorder began to increase. This situation brought about the development of organized metropolitan policing agencies. In 1833, Philadelphia enacted an ordinance (repealed, however, two years later) providing for a 24-man police force for daylight policing and a 120-man night watch.

Other cities attempted to use this same organizational model with separate day and night watches. But because separate administrators supervised each watch, rivalries and disputes were frequent. The New York legislature in 1844 passed a law creating the first unified policing system, and ten years later, Boston followed this lead. Soon all major cities had a similar system of policing.

This evolution in police organization, however, did little to resolve policing problems. New York at the time of the Civil War, for example, was viewed as the most crime-ridden city in the world, and other eastern cities were nearly as troubled by crime.[2] In fact, many of those problems, including unreasonable political control, still exist today.

The development of American policing in areas other than major cities was quite different. In many railhead and cow towns of the nineteenth century, a sheriff was selected by the town council. In some cases, he was nothing more than a hired gunman, since the council, recognizing the threat to the town's businesses by rowdy cowboys, and the difficulty of shopping in town, would hire the toughest man their money could buy. So in a few towns, someone like television's Matt Dillon was hired to "clean up" the city. Once it was cleaned up, a local man could be appointed sheriff.

In other areas, people relied upon a type of state police, like the Texas Rangers or the military. Los Angeles, for example, in the late 1700s was under the rule of Mexico, and its streets were patrolled by armed sentinels. Yet, as has been observed, the military was not very effective at bringing about social order. By 1836, the problem had become so serious that the citizens of Los Angeles decided to create their own public safety law. Those who committed serious crimes were no longer sent to Mexico City for trial; instead, they were taken to the plaza and shot.

[2]Arthur Charles Cole, *Irrepressible Conflict, 1859–1865, A History of American Life* (New York: Macmillan, 1934), Vol. III, pp. 154–55.

During the 1850s, Los Angeles became a true "boom town." It was the beef capital of the state and a mining center, so it attracted cattlemen, miners, storekeepers—and bandits. In 1851, Los Angeles selected its first city marshal; however, the city still continued to have the problems of lawlessness and mob violence. From a marshal system, the city moved to a guard system, and finally, in 1876, established a separate police department.

While much of the early history of law enforcement in Los Angeles reflects vigilante action, it was nonetheless a force interested in protecting the city. It was a type of western legal system that was unique to its time, the type of system that can exist without proper organization or legal status. Unlike England, which had already developed its system, the American West was still seeking one. By 1890, Los Angeles was beginning to utilize some of the policing methods of major eastern cities.

Between the latter part of the nineteenth century and the 1960s, American policing changed in many ways, owing principally to the development of technical advancements and the addition of more personnel. But organizationally, the police continued to meet the needs of their communities as they had with the watch and ward system.

From Sir Robert Peel we have developed four areas that have particular cogency to our times. I have, for the last seven years, preached their application both within my own police department and within my own community.

I have asked my policemen and my community to accept certain truths about their relationship with one another: I have demanded that my police officers accept a certain amount of the responsibility for the crime that occurs in our city but that the community acknowledge that its members share in that responsibility; I firmly believe that the police cannot function in a democratic society without the approval of the people they serve, and that the relationship that exists between the two is a truly sensitive one. A free people would not tolerate for too long a police agency that was brutal or one that gave preference to one faction or another. These Davis extensions of Peel are made with the deepest respect and devotion to his principles. They have particular applicability to us now.

2

Police Effectiveness

PHILOSPHY AND MEASUREMENT OF POLICE EFFECTIVENESS

The purpose and philosophy of the police in their role as servants of the people has never been fully developed. Police effectiveness involves the deterrence of crime, the apprehension of offenders, and the recovery of property. The police mission also calls for the prevention of crime. This is generally viewed as a more constructive role of the police, yet of all these objectives, prevention receives the least amount of attention in terms of resources and funding. Considerable resources have been committed to the collection and analysis of evidence, for example, but because of an inability to get a real handle on police productivity, other measurements of police effectiveness have generally failed.

In the evaluation of the effectiveness of a police agency, data on arrests and citations are relied upon heavily. However, the use of such measurements as the sole basis for effectiveness is inaccurate and tends to distort quality considerations as part of the variables. Likewise, such reliance fails to address the relationship of those statistical measures to the real problem of crime. Historically, in my own agency, such data gathering has been referred to as the "numbers game."

There has never really been any serious attempt to fully develop the philosophy of police effectiveness. For the police to be effective, it is absolutely vital that they know who they are and what their prime objective is. And the prime objective must be viewed as the prevention of crime.

Prime objective of Police

The British police set forth very succinctly the principle that the measure of police effectiveness is the absence of crime and the presence of public peace. Now, both these qualities are relative. There is no place on earth that has a total absence of crime and absolute peace. But a place that is relatively free of crime, where people live without constant fear of crime, is a place that is peaceful in that the people are able to express themselves and enjoy freedom. They can protest, or go about their shopping, without the fear that mobs or individuals will threaten them, and that is one test of police effectiveness.

In this age, there is an accountancy term currently in fashion. People are asked what the "bottom line" is in a certain situation, meaning the final result or, in the case of a business, the amount of profit or loss. For the police, the "bottom line" is the absence of crime and the presence of peace. In effect, then, whether or not the police are doing a good job depends on how much crime there is.

Police Effectiveness

FACTORS IN CRIME PREVENTION

The problem of crime has several dimensions, of course, and therefore it is not totally a police problem. One dimension relates to the nature of the populace—how crime-prone are they? For instance, it is fairly obvious that if the average age of the population were over 60 and the people were relatively impaired physically, there certainly would not be as many athletic burglars as there would be if the population were younger and more physically able. So there are some social factors that make a difference in the level of crime.

By and large, the greatest number of people who require police attention because of their criminal misconduct are between the ages of 14 or 15 and 29. This is known as the crime-prone age group. In my own agency, we found a few years ago that the median age of burglars was around age 15. That is, half our burglars were over 15 and half were under 15. So the character of a young person is a factor in the level of crime. In other words, if the home institution and the school institution have broken down, this fact reflects a dimension in crime that is outside the limits of police control. After all, we can't put a police officer in every home. In the final analysis, the family and other social institutions must be a significant factor in molding character and providing needed guidance.

The courts also have an effect on crime, because they are involved in handling the people the police apprehend. The role of the courts in the criminal justice system is discussed in another part of this book. My own view is that the police have the capability of controlling about 50 percent of all crime, but that the other half has causes and conditions over which the police should not be expected to have any direct control. The courts play a significant part in that half.

Therefore, an increase in crime in America is a reflection of many things. It indicates a failure of the family, a

15

failure of the schools, and a failure of other social institutions that are responsible for generating character. It is also a failure of the criminal justice system, including judges, probation officers, prosecutors, and correction supervisors. And it is also a failure of the police if they have not understood or responded to the problem. Since the police share responsibility for a portion of crime, it is logical that one measurement of their effectiveness should be how well they do in controlling and reducing it.

Recently, I participated in a quite lengthy discussion among several police chiefs on this subject. Some of the chiefs believed that the police should be able to explain away crime increases by pointing the finger at someone else. It is difficult to accept any accountability with regard to crime, but that is what must be done. In evaluating the effectiveness of the police, it is absolutely necessary to hold the police accountable for some of a crime increase.

So in measuring the effectiveness of a police agency, or of its police chief or sheriff, the level of crime is one of the factors that must be considered. When this factor becomes one of the measures of police effectiveness, a reduction of crime becomes a goal. This goal will be internalized because it poses certain negative consequences to the person or people being measured. The acceptance of a measurement standard related to crime can thus be used to form a regular analysis and evaluation process and make police resources more responsive. It can also promote cooperation among other criminal justice elements rather than isolating them within their own specialty.

CITIZEN RESPONSIBILITY

The police cannot operate effectively without citizen support. It is sad that so many of our citizens—and too many police officials—do not know that. Every citizen, not just the full-time police professional, has the responsibility to see that the laws are enforced. We will never achieve effective peace and safety if we depend merely upon the police profession to accomplish the task.

Partnership With the Police

There must be a partnership between the public and the police and a full realization that the public *are* the police and the police *are* the public. If the American police ever view themselves as something different from the rest of society, as they do in many parts of the world, this nation will be in trouble.

But even in this country, some police officers feel that they are members of a small minority group, misunderstood and unappreciated, that has had to take on all the problems of the world. Actually, nearly every policeman has felt just that way at some time, and he knew he wasn't alone. Interestingly, once we began to understand the Peelian principle that the people are the police and the police are a part of the people, we knew that we were not isolated, that we had everyone to help us in carrying out the task of policing society. It wasn't just us against the bad guys in the world. Some basic arithmetic might better show what I mean.

First, we should ask how many "bad people" there are in prison in a particular county or state—200, 500, perhaps 1,000. Then look at what the population of the county or state is. Perhaps the figure is 200,000, 500,000, a million, or as many as 5 million people. Let's say that you have 1,000 convicts in prison and a population of 800,000. If 10 percent of the total population were bad enough to be locked up, you would have 80,000 people in prison. So we know it can be demonstrated that the number is less than ten percent; in fact, less than one-half of 1 percent of the population is dangerous enough to other people to require imprisonment. Those who would assault someone unnecessarily or murder are a very small percentage of the whole population.

But let's speculate that those prison figures are much too conservative; they probably are. Let's say that 1 or 2 percent of the population should be in prison. That hardly justifies going around with an attitude of distrust and pessimism.

This is a problem that I will talk about in more detail later; right now, let me just emphasize the point that people must believe that they *are* the police and the police *are* the people. It must be realized that 99 out of 100 people are pretty good, as far as obeying the most serious laws is concerned. If you believe that, it will be easier to develop a partnership with almost everyone. And that makes sense. If the police officer thinks it through for himself, he will find that he can take into partnership the vast bulk of the people, and that the great majority of the people are good. A community might find itself with a better self-image if it went through the same exercise.

True enough, some people will gamble a bit. They might cheat against some law; they might go through a boulevard stop sign; they might become involved in some vice activity. But those people are not really "bad" in terms of hurting other human beings. In fact, they are more frequently victims. All of them are potential partners of the police. And interestingly, those people are probably more concerned than the police are in working together to provide a safer community. As a police administrator, my first goal was to prove this to policemen, to get them to understand the British philosophy that was thought out so well by Sir Robert Peel and his successors and is believed very firmly today in England.

Britain (except perhaps for Northern Ireland) is relatively safe today, 150 years after establishing its police system. The people are safe because they believe in this basic principle. The average Englishman is a very good fellow and, believe me, so is the average American. Once we come to this conclusion, that the police should be the people and the people should be the police, we can bring the forces within a community together and really turn them on.

Reverence for the Law

Abraham Lincoln delivered a speech in 1838 in Springfield, Illinois, when he was still just a young legislator. He said, in part:

> I hope I am over-wary; but if I am not, there is now an ill omen amongst us. I mean the increasing disrespect for the law which pervades the country. Accounts of outrages committed by mobs form the every-day news of the times.
>
> The question recurs, "How shall we fortify against it?" The answer is simple.
>
> Let every American, every lover of liberty swear never to violate in the least particular, the laws of the country and never to tolerate their violation by others. Let every man remember that to violate the law is to tear the character of his own and his children's liberty. Let reverence for the laws be breathed by every American mother to the baby . . . on her lap. Let it be taught in schools, and in colleges. Let it be written in primers and spelling books. Let it be preached from the pulpit, proclaimed in legislative halls and enforced in courts of justice. And in short, let reverence for the law become the *political religion* of the nation. If a state of feeling such as this shall universally, or even very generally prevail throughout the nation, vain will be every effort and fruitless every attempt to subvert our national freedom.

There are now more than 212 million people in this country. If each person decided, selfishly, egotistically, and immaturely, which laws he would obey or reject, how soon we would be reduced to anarchy!

Everyone professes to be *against* sin and *for* virtue, motherhood, the flag, and apple pie. With equal alacrity, everyone professes a reverence for the law and justice. This is perhaps valid in regard to crimes such as murder, robbery, and rape. But how deep is this well of reverence in reality?

19

How many people become queasy at the prospect of an audit of their income tax? How many utilize the rearview mirror in their car not so much for safety as for detecting the approach of a police car as they knowingly exceed the speed limit? How many fail to report criminal offenses and solemnly rationalize with comments like, "I'm minding my own business," or, "I don't want to get involved." A young girl in New York was brutally stabbed to death in view of more than 30 witnesses, none of whom attempted to give her aid or summon the police. While it may be dangerous to generalize on the basis of a few examples, the question cannot help but arise, "How deeply rooted is our reverence for the law?"

To generate reverence for the law, we must generate interest in the machinery of the law. Citizens must take a keen interest in whom they elect to judgeships, whom they elect as their prosecutors, and whom they elect at the executive level of government to direct or oversee the executive functions of the law. Individuals and groups must force the subject of future legislation as a major area of discussion into the dialogue between two candidates seeking a legislative position.

Again, we can turn to the wisdom of Abraham Lincoln for a realistic appraisal of this acceptance of the philosophy of the rule of law:

> When I so pressingly urge a strict observance of all the laws, let me not be understood as saying there are no bad laws, nor that grievances may not arise, for the redress of which, no legal provisions have been made. I mean to say no such thing. But I do mean to say that, although bad laws, if they exist, should be repealed as soon as possible, still while they continue in force, for the sake of example, they should be religiously observed. So also in unprovided cases. If such arise, let proper legal provisions be made for them with the least possible delay; but, till then, let them, if not too intolerable, be borne with. There is no grievance that is a fit object of redress by mob law.

To some, the law is just a game. They say, "I'm going to break the speed limit . . . I'm going to gamble, or do whatever

I want to do for myself.'' As a result of such thinking, we are in danger of losing the kinds of unified societal norms very necessary to look up to, standards to revere. Where there are no societal inhibitions against infractions of the law, a breakdown can occur. In turn, the police must constantly merchandise the concept of reverence for the law. When we do, we forestall that breakdown and encourage a community partnership that works toward that reverence.

3

The Professional Policeman

Both in the early years of my professional career and now, as I near the end of it, I have watched the emergence of one of the most energetic and determined movements toward professionalism of any class of working people I know. I have been proud to be a part of that movement.

It is not my purpose here to argue the subject of whether police work really is a profession. It has been my experience that those who belong to the "true" professions frequently demonstrate the most abysmal ignorance of ethical responsibilities. Likewise, their professional associations are capable of flagrant abuses when it comes to censuring the misconduct of their members. We have witnessed this in the political arena.

This discussion will center on the realities of bringing the police up to a standard of conduct that can be a credit to our communities and produce a standard of justice we can all understand and appreciate.

That standard of conduct has not always been so respectable. In my own early career, the police service had a dismal reputation. It has taken years of hard work, public education, and significant change by the police themselves to bring about the favorable reputation the police possess today. The balance has been tipped in spite of the efforts of radical groups that would destroy the kind of healthy relationship the American people want with their police.

Today, the police profession is close to achieving what we, in those early days, thought could be achieved—a high level of dedicated, impartial service by motivated people. There still exists a need for greater professional improvement, and as long as it is not impeded, through unrealistic demands initiated by militant employee unions or other obstacles, this too will be achieved.

STATUS OF THE PROFESSION

One of the strongest recommendations made by the President's Commission on Law Enforcement and the Administration of Justice in 1967[1] and repeated by the National Advisory Commission on Criminal Justice Standards and Goals in 1973[2] was the need to upgrade and professionalize the police service. Each of these studies recognized that the police are caught in a rapidly changing society that requires an increase in knowledge and skill. It has also been observed

[1] President's Commission on Law Enforcement and Administration of Justice, *Task Force Report: The Police* (Washington, D.C.: U.S. Government Printing Office, 1967), pp. 120–33.

[2] National Advisory Commission on Criminal Justice Standards and Goals, *Task Force on Police* (Washington, D.C.: U.S. Government Printing Office, 1973), pp. 9–44.

that the police, as an institution, suffers no more from the void created by social change than do other service-oriented agencies, especially within the public sector.

The subject of police professionalism may seem, to those viewing the police world from the outside, to be nothing more than an intellectual exercise in rhetoric. After all, many occupational groups besides the police are concerned about the achievement and maintenance of professional status. Further, since there are more than 25,000 police agencies in America, some might find it easier than others to achieve professional status. Such a possibility may raise the question of whether the whole field of law enforcement can achieve the goal of professionalism. The existence of numerous articles and reports, both officially and unofficially acknowledged, indicates that there is more than a passing interest in this area.

Many changes have been made in the field of law enforcement since the 1930s. In seeking greater efficiency, the police service has evolved from the image of the beat cop to that of a radio-dispatched mechanized service. But there remains a question as to whether this change has assisted in the reduction of crime, and in some areas of this country, interest has recently been shown in a return to the earlier model. The beat cop might not be able to do as much, the argument runs, but what he does accomplish is done very well, and most important it is done in a personal manner.

Then, some critics of law enforcement say that the structure and function of the police are unimportant, because the roots of crime are related to socioeconomic factors that are generally outside the sphere of police influence. Although there might be some basis for such observations, the fact remains that no other institution besides the police can provide the service so vital to the order of a free society. When the police service in a given area has been disrupted, people have suffered greatly.

Therein lies the challenge to the police—to save the public from the tragic results of crime. When someone needs a cop, there is little intelligent reason to sit down and determine the sociological basis of such need. The horror on our streets is real, and the average police officer does not have time to study hidden motivations before acting.

CHARACTERISTICS OF A PROFESSION

An essential ingredient for the achievement of professional status by any occupation is knowledge of the characteristics granted to such recognition. Let us begin with a definition of these characteristics. Richard H. Hall has suggested five attitudinal attributes of a profession that he believes are crucial.[3]

* A professional uses his professional organization as a major source of ideas and judgment. Both the formal organization and informal colleague groupings may serve this purpose. The American Bar Association and the American Medical Association might be viewed as the model for lawyers and doctors. Perhaps the International Association of Chiefs of Police is the model for law enforcement.

* A professional believes that he is performing a service to the public that is indispensable and is of equal benefit to himself.

* A professional believes in self-regulation. He feels that the persons best qualified to judge his work are within the profession. He believes that control within the profession is both desirable and practical.

* A professional has a sense of calling to his field. He is dedicated to his work and feels that he would probably continue in his effort even if there were fewer extrinsic rewards. (Since most policemen get relatively little financial reward for their work, this subject is somewhat moot. However, the financial rewards will be discussed in a later chapter.)

[3]Richard H. Hall, *Occupations and the Social Structure* (Englewood Cliffs, N.J.: Prentice-Hall, 1969).

* The professional believes he should have autonomy in his work. He feels that the practitioner must be allowed to make decisions without unnecessary external pressures. This includes pressures by external groups like clients and political representatives as well as pressures within the organization itself, which might well include those from the chief and his subordinate managers.

There are, of course, other characteristics of a profession—such as an expressed body of knowledge, specific educational and training standards, and a code of ethical conduct—but none of these factors automatically ensures recognition of professional status.

Within any organization, there are members who resist any change in their occupational or personal lives. They feel comfortable with their personal range of skills and they feel threatened by a move toward professionalism, which might question previous successes and methods. Further, as professionalism increases, educational demands also increase. Older members of the organization who have less education than newer members may perceive themselves as being in a relatively unfavorable position. Such organizational problems can create resistance and fragmentation, which can have serious consequences for the process of professionalization. The qualifications of some officers might then be viewed as more professional than those of others, but the organization itself might not achieve any higher status.

An additional factor in the professional status of an occupation is how it is perceived by others. The police have traditionally been viewed as being on the bottom of the status ladder. The police deal with judges, lawyers, physicians, teachers, and social workers, and they are always in an inferior position in their relative status—perhaps because police officers are generally paid less and are viewed as being in a less desirable field than the others. And although many surrounding professions and groups may appear to be enthusiastic about the professionalization of the police, this enthusiasm diminishes as the police begin to emerge as a

27

professional group. Some professionals view the police as little more than the collectors of human refuse.

Dr. Karl Menninger once observed:

> It should not be very hard to persuade a policeman to agree that his job requires him to have the ability of a superman. As a matter of fact, in choosing his profession, he has elected to be a superman. What he has said is that he wishes to announce himself ready to act more forcefully, more wisely, more calmly, more bravely, and more law-abiding than the average man. . . . Are these qualities appreciated by the public? Most certainly not. But let me ask you, too, if they are appreciated by the policemen themselves? When police officers come to have a higher opinion of themselves, to recognize that they are leaders in the community (the conscience of the community as it were), umpires in the great game of semi-domesticated human beings trying to live peaceably with one another in a complicated world, they will inspire similar respect, support, and admiration from the public at large.[4]

Law enforcement has responded to rapid social changes, and it has, for the most part, met the challenges. However, some of the requirements of professionalism remain for the future leaders of the police service.

IMPARTIAL POLICE SERVICE

One of the Peelian principles in which I have placed great faith is the impartial service of the police to the law. Regardless of what one individual or another thinks about the law, whether it is a good or a bad law, whether the law should be on the books or not, the professional police officer has the responsibility to enforce the law. It is not up to the

[4]Karl Menninger, *A Psychiatrist's World* (New York: Viking Press, 1950), pp. 750–53.

police to decide which laws will be enforced and which will not. Supreme Court Justice Thurgood Marshall made that point quite forcefully on behalf of blacks long before his appointment to the Court. He said that if a law was bad, it was up to the people to decide that, not the police.

Some laws receive more resources for their enforcement than others do, but this application of resources is not made because the police disagree with a particular law. Relative judgments are always made about the expenditure of resources. But there must be an absolutely impartial service to the law regardless of a policeman's personal thoughts about it.

So the decision about what should be a crime and what should not is a matter for the people, through their franchise and the initiative process; for the legislatures, through the legislative process; and for the elected chief executive, through his veto or signing power. It is not a police responsibility. As a result, the police should never have to apologize for enforcing any law.

Now, there has been great pressure in America to get police not to enforce certain kinds of law—the so-called victimless-crime philosophy. But the principle I have cited says that you enforce a law not because it pleases you, but because it has not been removed from the statute books. The victimless-crime myth is a dangerous fallacy! The police enforce the law because it is on the books, and they do not have to explain to anyone why they do it. *The reason they enforce the law is that it is the law.*

The concept of impartial service is important to the professionalism of the American police service because it gives validity to the separation of powers that has been designed into our system of government, and because it lifts the police service out of the political process. It is true that on occasions, the American police service has not kept itself from becoming mired in the most degrading of political involvements. But the principle remains. It remains for those who wish to use it, to look upon it for guidance, and to call upon it for strength when the temptation to stray becomes too strong.

THE USE OF FORCE

Minimum Force

The British also have a principle that says that force should be a last resort for the police; that first we should do everything within our power to handle a situation through persuasion. That means that we should attempt to "sell" someone on doing what is necessary, whether it is submitting to arrest or discontinuing a particular violation of the law. This concept of exhausting every other means of persuasion, diplomacy, and salesmanship before it becomes necessary to use force was fundamental in the mind of Sir Robert Peel. He saw it as being one of the basic differences between a domestic and a military peace-keeping force.

The use of persuasiveness should always come before the use of force. Some policemen, like some other people, have difficulty with this concept; when they put a badge on, they get offended if anyone displays resistance or doesn't show respect. They may have a rather natural human reaction to abandon persuasiveness and use force.

Never should force be used merely as retribution for how someone talked to a policeman, or for what someone did. If policemen find it difficult to adhere to this basic principle, they should not be policemen. When force does have to be used, it should be in only the reasonable minimum amount necessary. The professional policeman must be expected to use only the degree of force that will accomplish a particular purpose.

Sadly, there are some who cannot use restraint in the application of force; when that happens, a police department is in trouble. The standard for the application of force must be the minimum amount necessary to control the person or take him into custody. And that does not mean that an officer is required to place himself in peril according to his judgment and the conditions.

One of the most serious areas of concern that some of

us have had relates to the application of weaponless self-defense techniques to law enforcement. People can be trained in aikido and other forms of the self-defense disciplines to enable them to handle almost any situation. However, the philosophy that goes along with the art is extremely difficult to instill into people. Also a person's self-confidence can be built up while he is in training, but if he fails to practice the art, he soon resorts to the most basic type of force. Or if he misapplies a technique and it fails to work, he blames the self-defense method and begins to use some other form of force. That is a management problem that can really have an impact on an agency's whole philosophy of force.

The Order of Force

In addition to the use of only the minimum amount of force reasonably necessary, there must also be an *order of force*—that is, clearly understood levels of force available for different situations, so that the police win the altercations and the bad guys lose—and that means that the citizenry wins as well. The order of force begins with an individual officer's use of physical restraint—including, besides his own physical strength, his weapons, such as a baton and guns, and perhaps other devices.

The next level of force involves other policemen, such as the officer's partner and other responding police units—preferably marked squad cars, each containing a pair of policemen. The idea is to assemble a massive response when you need it; when several marked police cars swarm in on a situation, it should be pretty clear to those interested in breaking the law that they don't have a chance. Helicopters, of course, add greatly to that response. In Los Angeles, we use turbine helicopters with a top speed of about 150 miles an hour, which reduces the response time appreciably. Such a massive show of force frequently eliminates the need for any other action at all. It most assuredly results in fewer lives lost, by police and citizens alike.

response time.

The Professional Policeman

There must next be a special force capability that is held back until it is absolutely needed. If something cannot be handled by police in a local area in Los Angeles, we call in our Metropolitan Squad, which can be redeployed right in the middle of a watch. This squad consists of about 200 men, a very small percentage of our department, who can be thrown into an area and just inundate it. The word soon gets out, and the burglars and robbers and gangsters realize they cannot fool around with our policemen. Just the knowledge of such police presence eliminates a great deal of the need for physical force.

Our next level of force would be our Special Weapons and Tactics Team—SWAT. Television has made these men famous—or infamous, if you like. This select group is designed to cope with people who like to use guns and bombs. The idea is to put into operation people who are bigger and tougher and sharper and better trained and better shots than the criminals—people who can be thought of as invincible. Certainly we want the real baddies to think that.

Our SWAT teams train at Camp Pendleton Marine Corps Base and work out very strenuously indeed. They can climb up and down walls, if need be, and, if they have to, place plastic explosives that will blow up an entire building. They are tremendous, both physically and mentally. If any group of lawbreakers wants to play games with these guys, they are even dumber than we think.

Thus, in Los Angeles we have developed an order of force from the individual policeman up through other specialized units, including heavy weaponry. The idea is that our people do not lose. I doubt that the next paramilitary revolutionary group that arises is going to decide to come to the city of Los Angeles. The SLA decided that they didn't like it worth a damn.

A police department must have, like a military unit, a minimum level of force and then successive levels that are progressively stronger. If the agency does not have this capability, it must be developed.

4

Police Organizations

POLICE UNIONISM AND
PROFESSIONAL ASSOCIATIONS

As a former police-association representative, I have strong feelings about such groups. A chief of police and his police officers can only benefit from taking part in organizations within their profession. They must share their problems and successes. They must work to overcome the failures of their peers in other parts of the country. This participation is important, because few things occur just once. It seems that there is a regular progression of police problems that frequently start on one side of the country and within two or three years envelop all departments in the United States. No police executive can afford to take an "I am strictly management" viewpoint of his relationship with his policemen.

Frequently, however, a police employee problem cannot be solved by talking to professional colleagues in other parts of the country, because they may not have faced the problem. For example, when police unionism became very strong in the sixties on the East Coast, we learned that the policemen involved in the union movement were not so much interested in salary increases and benefits; they were mainly concerned with management rights, such as the authority to administer lie detector tests. They wanted to get these rights away from management, and some succeeded. We had never come up against this situation, but that is exactly what is happening in the rest of the country today. Those of us who learned the lesson held onto management prerogatives; those who were not listening were taken to the cleaners.

Even though the critical issues have frequently, of late, been about management rights and working conditions, police associations have always involved themselves in the basic wage and benefits issues. With only a few exceptions, Los Angeles being a notable one, police officers have been generally unsuccessful in securing long-lasting, comprehensive compensation programs. Generally, cities and towns have used their emergency services as a means to economize, and police officers have been unable to bring about significant salary or benefit improvements through their own efforts.

Since this is the case, and since our government officials have generally failed to provide equitable compensation, the only way that compensation is being improved is through appropriate employee representation units, some of which are affiliated with nonpolice unions, some of which are not. Many police associations are not strictly unions; they are more like guilds, made up exclusively of peace officers. It is my own opinion that police unions should not be affiliated with organized labor because of the potential for conflict of interest. Policemen have to maintain order during labor strikes, and they should not be on the side of either labor or management. They need to have as much objectivity as possible. The whole concept of a strike is partisanship, and such thinking is totally inimical to an impartial police service.

Also, since unions engage very heavily in the political process, educating voters and lobbying politicians, policemen should remain as far away from such ventures as possible. If police associations become a closely aligned part of regular trade unions, there is a great possibility that two things will happen: first, that the police will become unnecessarily embroiled in politics and other areas that have no pertinence to the police; and second, since policemen are fewer in number than some other parts of the working population represented by the unions, that they will be a minority in the unions and will necessarily be required to subordinate their interests to the majority. For these reasons, police associations should be absolutely independent of organized labor.

But just as important, police administrators must look on police "unions" as a fact of life and not resent them. In great part, they were brought about by the failure of chiefs and city managers, and of mayors and councilmen and chambers of commerce, and of citizens as a whole, to address the issue of police compensation and working benefits. It is absolutely proper that police officers have a voice, an organization that can work for them to get appropriate compensation. Police administrators must believe strongly in the right of police officers to be represented by their own association. As strongly as I believe that policemen should not affiliate with organized labor—and I have actively sought legal constraints to prevent them from exercising the traditional union tool of the right to strike—I also believe that their right to associate must not be infringed.

There is great value in maintaining a strong professional association. Those involved learn the answers; but more important, they learn the problems. I have seldom come away from meetings with my association with precise answers that might be readily adapted to a particular problem, but the important aspect of this process is the discussion of problems and the definition of each.

There are, for example, some things that all police

associations should have as basic conditions: There should be some kind of formula to see that salaries are adjusted annually; and there should be survey and measurement methods to ensure that police pay and fringe benefits are appropriate. It is such provisions that demonstrate good faith to police officers and go a long way toward preventing greater demands in other areas.

In exchange for basic considerations, I think there should be statutes defining it as a crime for any police officer to strike. A police officer who strikes after being given basic guarantees for a decent wage and benefit structure should be discharged from the service and criminally prosecuted. On two occasions, we tried to secure such a measure in Los Angeles. Yet each time, the police union representatives actively lobbied against it. It would be good for the policemen and good for the community to have such a restraint; but the association is, of course, concerned about the impact of such legislation on its power. If wages and salaries were officially handled in an objective and legal manner, the general membership might soon decide that it no longer needed a union. The members could save a great deal of money in dues, but the union directors would lose their major reason for existence. A "no-strike" law coupled with prevailing-wage provisions would provide some protection for policemen by giving them a realistic means for proper compensation. At the same time, the community would be assured of no police strike problems. Everyone would win under such a system, except, of course, the union, which might find it difficult to justify an increase in dues for lobbying purposes only.

It is incumbent on the chief executive to work with employee unions just as he might work with any other organization. Police chiefs work with other unions for the purpose of getting along with all the parties and having labor peace, and police unions should be treated in the same manner.

Beyond working with unions, the management of police departments should take the initiative to have appropriate benefits guaranteed. It is one of their management obligations to see that their people are properly compensated. If the working benefits other than pay, the so-called fringe benefits, are totally out of line with those of the rest of society, then police management should take an active role in having them brought up to date. If police salary scales are inappropriate to the jobs being performed, then police management should take the initiative in seeing that there are adequate scales of compensation.

As I mentioned before, very few places in the world properly categorize their police officers. They are thrown into one big pot with all the other personnel and they are all paid the same, even though they may have vastly different jobs to perform. Those with more complicated jobs, requiring more skill, more experience, and higher selection criteria, are not properly compensated. But the unions seldom concern themselves with such matters; they are too interested in power and politics. There should be someplace to go within police work without becoming a supervisor, and there should be a successful, gratifying career path for professional police officers—and police unions should be involved in these matters. Police unions have a responsibility to take up and support the cause for proper classification and proper compensation, and to take part in representation of policemen's needs to the governing bodies of their city or county or state—and without utilizing strikes or other methods of cutting back police services.

POLICE UNION ACTIVISM

The police strikes that we have witnessed in recent history were not necessarily caused by policemen's believing that they were underpaid. Certainly the New York City work stoppage in the early seventies was not caused by dissatisfaction with the salary level of the working policemen, because New York has the highest-paid police agency in the nation.

Police strikes occur because police officers elect people

to head their organizations who, in this day and age, seem to have as their campaign slogan, "To hell with the brass." The campaigns amount to, "Vote for me and I'll punch all the brass in the nose. I'll keep the chief of police down so he won't be able to investigate you or discipline you; and when I'm elected, if you have any grievances about where you are assigned, come and see me. I'm running on an anti-brass platform that will take grievances up to the highest courts." As a result, we have seen many radicals instead of statesmen elected to head police associations.

Police unionism is a new phenomenon, but it parallels the increase in public-employee unionism throughout America. I know what I'm talking about, because I was there for seven years. I did all this work, but we had a different type of philosphy then. We worked with people who were concerned about balance. Our actions had to be good for the department, they had to be good for the people, and they had to be good for policemen.

Police unions today, like teachers' unions and other public-service unions, are saying, "We're going to declare war on city government, the city council, the chief adminis- trator, and the rest of the brass." Each association tries to outdo the others in terms of wage demands and union organi- zation. Policemen vote in the most radical guy that can be found, and when they find he is not radical enough, they throw him out and vote for someone else who promises greater victories over management—and who is in turn thrown out two years later for the same reason. Few police union representatives last very long. Yet their common program is to knock the brass, and they meet occasionally at the national level and talk about their chiefs and their departments.

But not for one moment has our most recent strike activity simply involved a matter of pay. The police unions are preoccupied with management prerogatives—transfers and demotions and such. What those in the union movement forget is that the police service has a basic responsibility to the public. In fact, the public has been more generous to its policemen than to most of its public servants. Los Angeles is an excellent example.

The issue, it would appear, is power. Those in the union movement want to get into the driver's seat in our cities, and they want to do it outside the traditional chain of command. By using political power, the police union will, if unchecked, be able to undo most of the goodwill that has developed between the public and the police in America. Is there any case where policemen were starving to death?

In many cases, there were police agencies, only blocks away, making far less money than those who were striking—yet they hadn't threatened to walk off the job.

A decent salary structure *is* important. It is foolish to take a good man with 20 or 30 years of service and pay him the same rate as some kid who only has two years of experience. It is that kind of issue that the police unions should be fighting for, rather than the prerogatives of management. The public pays its government leaders to exercise their leadership. Those leaders need the latitude to make decisions, and not always popular ones at that. What has happened lately in the union movement is that management decisions are thwarted or stalled at the whim of union leaders who do not share the responsibilities to the public for providing police service.

A police chief has the responsibility to ensure that the police union does not misrepresent conditions to its membership. He must also do what he can to learn the needs of his personnel and, where possible, be responsive to them. In so doing, he must be true to the test discussed earlier: Every benefit must be considered in the light of how it affects the public, the agency, *and* the policemen.

The Jacobs Plan in 1971 solved the basic pay issue in my department. That, together with the salary-setting formula we secured in the 1950s, has reduced most union demands to either peripheral health and pension benefits or management issues. We don't have a recruitment problem. We have 5,000 people ready to join the LAPD today. People are lined up from Los Angeles to New York waiting for the opportunity to join. And almost certainly, we will not have a union problem similar to that experienced by other cities.

When I was traveling in England, it was brought to my attention that the English police officer receives very generous benefits, particularly in the form of housing allowances and a great deal of practically guaranteed overtime. It is these benefits that make the position very appealing. Oddly, at the time an English police officer retires, he has not accrued these benefits as a part of his retirement pay. In the United States, these types of benefits and another, the take-home car, have become important issues, which police unions have become aware of. But instead of pursuing these issues and trying to clarify them for the benefit of their membership, most unions are dissipating their time and their membership dues on specious lawsuits or speculative investment ventures. Until the union leaders begin to recognize this, they and their memberships will fall short of achieving the kinds of benefits that policemen truly want and deserve.

5

The Cost
of Policing

Among American cities, there is a vast difference in the number of police personnel per thousand population—the relative number of both sworn and civilian personnel hired for the purpose of getting the job done. Some police departments are run very effectively and efficiently with one officer, or two, per thousand. Many of them, like New York City, are run at nearly four officers per thousand and have been running that way for decades. Washington, D.C., at its recent peak, operated at almost six officers per thousand population. In view of this fact, our nation's police agencies should be rated not just on the level of crime or the amount of vice or the general level of peace in the city, but also on their cost per capita.

COST PER CAPITA

If the per capita cost of policing for a city is $50, the total for a family of four is $200 per year. This might be termed a police insurance policy. It isn't like a regular casualty policy, because such policy would financially reimburse its holder after something bad had happened; the police insurance policy works toward preventing something bad from happening. A police policy at $50 per capita or $200 per household is less than automobile insurance for the family car. So we can ask the average family, "Is the police service worth as much as the insurance policy on your car?" In other words, can the people afford to pay a decent wage to policemen?

The answer to the question, of course, lies in our sense of values; and the reasonable answer is, "Yes, we can afford to pay." Our policemen need not work for borderline poverty wages; we need not run a department that is understaffed; and police departments do not have to do without equipment. Most of the people in our cities and towns do not want to risk living in a jungle because of an inadequate level of police protection.

A per capita cost comparison is something that should be done for all cities, but no one has yet done such a study. There are many complicated factors involved in computing those cost figures. For one example, it is necessary to look at the cost of services of other, comparably sized departments. For another, a total cost figure for a police department might reflect a pension contribution that had not been made by the city for several years, and now the city might be playing catch-up. Such considerations must be determined when attempting to assess the real cost of operating a single department.

In addition, no two cities can really be totally compared. Every city is unique, and what it takes to police one city will not necessarily be the same in terms of dollars or manpower in another. But rough comparisons can be drawn if the cities are generally of the same size and type. It would be very suspicious to me if *any* city was successful in combatting crime with policing costs running below $50 per capita, or above $100 per capita.

Differences might be observed in the types of cities receiving the service. Care must be exercised in comparisons because of differences in the age of the population; the number of active persons; the number of attractive targets, as with a resort city; the value of homes; the wealth of families; and the topography. All must be considered. There is, for example, a difference in policing between mountainous areas where radio cars have to spend time driving up canyons to handle calls, and areas that are relatively flat.

All these factors must be considered before any final comparison; but the comparison should be made. My point is that police departments should be held accountable for their per capita cost of service. Ultimately, those costs must also be evaluated as to their relative success in preventing crime from adversely affecting a community. If the dollars being spent are not doing the job, and especially if the costs are relatively high, there is something wrong. But if crime is quite low even though costs are fairly high, residents of a city can be comfortable with the thought that they are getting their money's worth.

FISCAL RESPONSIBILITY—IT'S NOT PENNIES FROM HEAVEN

The most expensive personal service a city uses is almost always policing. The total cost may vary from city to city, but the budget for policing can account for 20 to 40 percent of a city's total budget. Further, 90 to 95 percent of that amount is generally set aside for salaries or salary-related expenses. So the police executive has the lion's share of the city's budget in his hands—but he usually takes it for granted. He assumes that he will get enough money and men each year. However, lately other people are starting to look very covetously at that police budget.

Very few people know anything about the nature of

police budgets anyway, including many who run police departments. Staying within a police budget is a very complex matter. It involves the art of using as few resources as possible and still maintaining a low crime rate and securing public peace. From personal experience, it is clear to me that very few politicians—including mayors—know much about the budgetary process. A budget for a police agency should not be part of some politician's gamesmanship; it is far too important to a city and to its people. Too often, the budget is used at election time to show the voters how "responsible" the candidate has been. Sometimes that "responsibility" is a mask for stupidity.

Police work is a type of service that is subjectively viewed by the public, and for that reason it is enormously important for the police administrator to be fiscally responsible. He must evaluate the need for every specific type of service that is performed. Costs must be constantly analyzed in terms of resources allocated; occasionally, when conducting this little exercise, he will come across services his agency provides that should not be part of the budget.

There is an example cited at some schools of public administration that makes the point. Some years ago in England, someone investigated an expenditure for a guard assigned to watch the English coastline. It turned out that the first guard was assigned in 1805 to watch for Napoleon's ships, and the guard duty was passed on to each succeeding generation. In 1958, a guard was still being assigned to this spot to watch for Napoleon. For the sake of my English forebears and the schools in Great Britain, I hope the man assigned at that time did not know what it was he was supposed to be watching for.

I pointed out earlier that most police departments are organized now in pretty much the same way they were organized 50 years ago. Perhaps they have added a community-relations division and an internal-affairs unit and one or two other specialized units, but otherwise they are about the same. It may well be that some of their functions are not necessary, at least to the same degree today as in the past.

It is important for each police agency to publish annually a statement of cost per capita for policing services. That statement should include the cost to the city of the services of other city departments that are used by the police service. For example, if the city's computer system is run by a data bureau and the costs of police use are passed on to the policing agency, they should be reflected in the total-cost figure.

The annual police report should contain all pertinent information—but none that is not pertinent. It is incredible the irrelevant stuff that sometimes gets into those reports. I have seen some that were crowded with the pictures of everybody on the police department, particularly the brass, just to get their faces seen. Some police departments inform their citizens through their annual reports what they are doing that is new, and what their long-term progress in crime prevention is. A few might highlight a youth program, or show some community-relations program. That is all well and good, and great public relations, but reports such as this may cost a lot of money to produce, and taxpayers may wonder what they are getting from the expenditure.

The effective leader owes it to himself and the people he serves to be conversant with the fiscal status of his agency. He has an obligation to himself and those people to keep them informed. If he does, he may even find that he has better luck getting added resources when he needs them.

II
POLICE LEADERSHIP

6

The Sources
of Leadership

There may be a professional career in business or in government that is more competitive than police work, but I can't think of one. Some professions have built-in competition, with several members vying for one position, but that is transitory; when the position is filled, the competition is over until the next time a position is open. Because of the inherent conflict in police work and the vital importance of the profession to the lives and safety of our citizens, the position of police leader is critical.

Even though I had some conflicts with him, it was my good fortune to have been under the leadership of Bill Parker, former chief of the Los Angeles Police Department, during the 1950s. He was clearly the man for his time, in that he possessed the leadership traits needed to do a very important job. That is by no means a chance thing. Somewhere along the line, the traits necessary to lead a large police organization also came my way. Some of my thoughts on the subject of leadership follow.

WHERE DO LEADERS COME FROM?

It has been my observation over the years that the best leaders are those who are sought out. Unfortunately, most of today's leaders are people who have pushed themselves forward. They are self-anointed, self-appointed, and self-ordained. In the police world, they want to be sergeants or lieutenants or captains for the sake of their egos, their own private motivations, higher pay, status, or whatever. Organizationally, police agencies have a responsibility to seek out the better-adjusted, more competent people and try to push them into positions of leadership. Otherwise, we will get a pretty poor crop.

In politics, for example, presidential candidates generally come from Congress, usually from the Senate, but how did they get there? Usually, *they* decided they wanted to be senators, and so *they* did all the things they had to do to get there. At least, the primary candidates seem to share this commonality. It would seem that we should have something better to offer the country. Why do we have to narrow ourselves down to members of Congress and a few governors in our selection of people to run the government of the United States of America? It is hard to imagine that Washington, D.C., can reflect our best leadership, but the process of self-anointment has its roots there.

As citizens, if we were more careful in selecting our councilmen, our state representatives, our congressmen, and our senators, we would live in a better world. And in the same way, in too many police agencies, we do nothing to encourage participation by the best people in the promotional process. We just put out a promotional notice and let whoever wants to come along run in the race. And if policemen were more careful about whom they selected to run their police associations, we would be much better off. In most instances, it is a case of self-selection and self-ordainment.

Police leaders should ask themselves if the people under them, the well-adjusted ones, are being encouraged to participate in the promotional process. Those men who seem to be satisfied just to do a good job should be approached, even though some of them will not be convinced that they should participate in the process. Digging out the real indigenous leaders and pushing them a little is better than permitting those who promote themselves to dominate the competition.

CHARACTERISTICS OF POTENTIAL LEADERS

There is already extensive research on where leaders come from. One of the findings most interesting to me is that leaders tend to be more persuasive and to have more intelligence than the average of their particular group.[1] It would appear that a group will not follow someone who is beneath them intellectually. However, the leader may not be the *most* persuasive or the *most* intelligent member of his group. It is almost always a combination of these and other factors that makes a leader.

Likewise, research has found that leadership is generally associated with a particular situation, rather than being a general thing. Seldom do people say, "I could follow that person anywhere. I agree with everything he says." The United States Army found, by observing men at work, that leadership was task-related. If a tank broke down, for example,

[1]For a contemporary view of leadership in today's world, see Michael Maccoby, *The Gamesman: The New Corporate Leaders* (New York: Simon & Schuster, 1976).

51

one type of guy would emerge as the leader. He would say to the others, "Wait a minute, we are not going to sit around and wait for somebody to come and rescue us tomorrow." He would take charge and get the tank repaired. In another kind of military situation, perhaps stressful combat, another kind of man would emerge as the leader. One person has the qualities to take command in a mechanical situation, another to lead in, let's say, a discussion group, and still another kind to get people to enthusiastically charge up a hill. The guy who is the leader in one situation is not necessarily the leader in every other situation. In other words, the army found that leadership is specific to the problem being solved.

There is no single test that is sufficiently comprehensive to measure whether one man has more potential as a leader than another. Because of the tremendous number of crises in police work, a certain type of field situation may be ideal for one high-ranking officer, whereas the management and supervision of a budget may require another man. Perhaps dealing effectively with the public would require still another leader. Seldom are all these qualities found in one man. In the selection of a leader, those factors have to be considered; the fellow being considered may not be effective in certain areas, but in other areas he may be outstanding. The chief executive must be willing, on balance, to accept the person's outstanding characteristics, at the same time realizing that the candidate is an imperfect human being.[2]

THE SELECTION PROCESS

During my career, there were some divisions I did not appreciate being assigned to, particularly computer work, even though I might have been more qualified for such work than some of my peers. I did not like being required to work

---

[2]Peter F. Drucker, *Managing for Results* (New York: Harper & Row, 1964).

with machines, and the last thing in the world I wanted was to have to learn all about computers. It was a pain in the neck then, but now I am glad that Bill Parker gave me that assignment in 1960. Not only did it become an asset to me in understanding the systems of today's world, but to this day, I still consider the feelings my people have about being assigned to a particular job. It should be one of the considerations in making selection decisions.

Ten years later, as chief, I discovered something that I think can be extremely important to the selection process. I used it for making a particularly important selection to a critical position, and I expect to use it from now on. It involves a type of peer-group selection, and it came about this way.

The last time we had a vacancy in the rank of assistant chief, which pays about $58,000 a year, I looked over the candidates for the position and found that there were several good men for the job. But which one should be chosen? While I had been sitting up at the top as chief, those men had been a couple of ranks down, at the deputy-chief level. I came to the conclusion that even though I had many perceptions about these people, a leader's ability to pick one of his immediate subordinates over another for an advancement is questionable.

Now, I may be a little bit different from most top leaders, in that I pick people as my immediate subordinates who I think should have my job, or who should develop the qualities necessary for my position. Frequently, chief executives will pick someone who is a "good old boy." A "good old boy" is someone who will protect the executive's backside, not compete with him; someone who will be loyal to him and provide him with gossip about others in the organization. But when I leave my organization, I want my replacement to be chosen from assistant chiefs who are the most eminently qualified men in the country. I want them to be able to compete very vigorously, so that my department will get the type of leadership it will need in the future, rather than the kind it might have if I had selected a bunch of "good old boys."

There is real chief's material down there, and I cannot be jealous of them or fear that they will pose a threat to me. A chief executive must commit himself to that sort of thinking, otherwise he will easily fall into the trap of picking a subordinate who is not threatening, someone who is going to be loyal to him regardless. The Nixon White House did it that way, and it was a disaster.

So what I did in this particular case was to evaluate the eleven potential candidates for that job in a special manner. Each one of them came in separately and was handed eleven cards, each with the name of a deputy chief on it. Each man was told that, because he lacked the objectivity to rate himself, we were going to eliminate his name in the exercise, except that at the end he could tell my why he thought he was qualified. We were there to play cards, and the session was private, just between us. The candidate was going to rank his ten peers in the order in which he thought they should be selected for the position. Each man was asked if he objected to this card game and was told that he didn't have to play.

I had already made my own choices for the top three people, and the group came in with very similar results. But in checking the cards, I found out something interesting: there are little things about a man's potential for leadership that people will not generally talk about. They may grumble to themselves, and they may talk to their fellow workers of the same rank, but they don't usually broadcast their feelings about that type of thing. So as each man made his selection, I asked why. I would scratch little notes and say, "You put so-and-so last; why?" Well, there was always one reason or another for the selection, some of which were amazing.

Each candidate in this peer-selection process was given a score ranging from 1 to 10, with 1 the highest possible rating and 10 the lowest. The scores were then totaled and averaged as a combined score. If a candidate got a final score of 10, he was last. Well, there was unanimity on the bottom two men and general unanimity on the top two. The top two had ratings of about 1.7 and 2. Then the scores dropped down to about 3.5. The "good old boys" were around 5, and the bottom two were very close.

When my selection was made this time, it was made with a lot more authority, because the consensus of the group from which I chose this man was that he was the best. The first and second men came out virtually equal; fortunately, I was able to appoint both of them. As a matter of fact, when I appointed the first one, I was not sure how it would work, but my doubts were soon laid to rest; he has performed just exactly the way everyone told me he was going to perform. There were other candidates that I might have taken a chance on, but the group rated them lower. They were viewed as having personal problems that interfered with their giving undivided attention to their work, or as not being comfortable in making decisions, or as wanting to get group support before decisions were made. You learn all kinds of things about a fellow from the wisdom of his peers.

If I were going to another police department to help that department select a chief of police from within the organization, I would sit down and play cards. Those men within the organization would pick the best man for the position. Some other very interesting things would be learned from this selection process, such as whether a person is manipulating his choices to put down a competitor and move himself up. In some cases, a candidate obviously knows that good old Soft-shoes really shouldn't be number 2, but he will put him there anyway, to force the real number 2 guy down a little, and that stands out like the glow of a sore thumb in a fog. There are a number of fascinating insights that can be gained through peer-group selection. A man may not know very much about the people a couple of ranks below him or those a couple of ranks above him, but people in the same rank know each other as well as they know the back of their hand.

I have not considered using this type of system for personnel evaluation reports, because I believe there would be some deficiencies. Consider for a moment the man who

55

works on the budget if the guy rating him is in the operations section. I do not believe that the man in operations is capable of rating him. He may know if the men are acting well with him and what his general qualities of leadership are, but can he really evaluate the quality of his work? Therefore, I believe a man's immediate superior can probably evaluate his performance much better. But the immediate superior cannot always evaluate the man's leadership potential; his peers can do a much better job with that.

I am sold on this method for selecting immediate subordinates. These decisions won't be made only by myself again, because even though I came to the same general conclusion, the advantages of the exercise cast those decisions in cement for me. If the selections had been at variance with mine, it would have been an excellent education for me.

Executives often make very distinct mistakes in their selection process. They select people they feel comfortable with, but pretty soon they find they cannot handle their choice. For instance, some people, when they are promoted, begin to think that they are the boss, and soon they cannot hear the real boss; their ego gets in the way. It is a problem of power and of handling power in the right way. A leader cannot let the power or status of his position interfere with the effectiveness of the organization. A man can be fully qualified, but if he cannot handle power, his organizational value in the management arena is limited. Some people get high on power, to the point that they don't get enough oxygen for the proper functioning of their brains. I have been fortunate in having some truly outstanding people work for me and with me. Each of them would be successful in almost any organization.

LEGAL SOURCES OF AUTHORITY

It is vital to leadership, and especially police leadership, that the chief executive and others know what their authority is and what their responsibilities and limitations are. The police leader must know these legal parameters; but for people to understand him and his decisions, it is more important that others know them.

There are various legal considerations contained in city charters, ordinances, and state laws, and sometimes in case law, that define legal authority. In California, for example, a police officer can make a misdemeanor arrest without a warrant only when the misdemeanor has occurred in his presence. A citizen who is the victim of a misdemeanor crime and is not familiar with the law may have difficulty understanding why the officer does not arrest the known violator. But unless that crime was observed by the officer, or unless the officer has a warrant, no police-initiated arrest may be made.

Similarly, one of the responsibilities of a police chief executive, mandated by law, is that if he discovers that a subordinate is dangerous to the public, he is required to remove him from employment. If he acts otherwise, he is personally responsible for any liability resulting from the actions or inactions of that man. This is the law in California, at least, and other states have similar statutes. So when a subordinate has repeatedly shown that he is brutal—for example, through the unnecessary application of force—the police chief executive has no alternative but to seek the removal of that man from the police service. If he fails to exercise that responsibility, then the chief must take the place of that man in terms of personal liability, and he may find that he is financially liable along with the jurisdiction that employs him. In knowing this about the responsibilities of their chief, subordinates may better understand why he takes certain disciplinary actions.

As a leader, the chief of police may have very little legal power. Under the Charter for the City of Los Angeles, for instance, the police commission is the head of the police department. It has virtually all the power and authority over the department. It can make the policy of the department and can overrule me on virtually anything. The only power granted to me by the Charter involved the ultimate use of discipline and decision in disciplinary matters. Some charters provide just the reverse. Some, for example, provide the police commission with all disciplinary authority and give the chief all other policy-making power. But in Los Angeles, the chief is required to seek approval from the Board of Police Commissioners when he wants to make any significant change in policy. The chief formally prepares a report to the board, has it placed on the agenda, and discusses it with the board before seeking to make it the official policy of the department.

Thus, there can be a trememdous difference between the power of the commissioner of police in New York City and the power of the chief of police in Los Angeles. In one case there is a great deal of power, in the other a relatively powerless figure. In order to be effective, each leader must be aware of his authority and learn how to use it effectively. I prefer the Los Angeles system, because it puts the police under responsible civilian control.

Before a person can do his job as a leader, he must possess a clear understanding of what his authority and responsibilities are. He cannot go anywhere until he knows the fundamental rules of the ballgame. And it is just as important that the public and the leader's subordinates fully understand those rules. The effective leader will pay attention to those details and develop that understanding within his organization and community.

7

Police Leadership and the Community

A leader in any field needs to have certain qualities to ensure his success. But as we saw in the preceding chapter, leadership is at least in part task-related, and since the job of a police leader involves so much interaction with his community, he needs to have a set of qualities appropriate to that job.

EDUCATION AND COMMUNICATIVE ABILITY

A police leader should have a better-than-average education, probably somewhat better than the average education of the people he is going to lead within the organization and

a police leader should have a better than average education somewhat better than the average education of the people he is charged with protecting outside the organization. The reason is not solely the benefit of the technical knowledge he may have acquired through the educational process, although this is necessarily one aspect. Technical knowledge is rather specific, and it can be obtained through home study, through life experience, or in other ways. But an education garnered through the formal process is essential to police leadership because it tends to vest the holder of a position of authority with the ability to empathize with people. To use an overworked word, education is broadening. It helps to provide an understanding of human nature and an ability to communicate.

One communication form is the English language, and most of us do a pretty poor job of using this single vehicle. Yet when we deal with people as managers or as leaders, communication will be one of the keys to success. It would be difficult for any leader to get his message across effectively if he lacks the ability to communicate his message to others.

AWARENESS OF WORLD EVENTS

A leader must also be constantly aware of what is going on in the world around him. That means he must read newspapers, periodicals, and other written material; and he must either watch or listen to regular news broadcasts. I have somebody read the *Los Angeles Times* for me and point out significant items, because I have to know what is in it. But a leader cannot depend totally on a staff to keep abreast of events. I have the *Wall Street Journal* delivered to my home; and I also subscribe to the *Village Voice,* a clearly unabashedly far-left publication out of New York. It lets me hear what the lastest rumblings are in the "here and now" liberal community. If you automatically adjust most of what you read in the *Voice* a little or a lot to the right, it is a great tabloid. It pulls no punches, and the *Voice* is concise. I've also subscribed to the *Washington Journal,* which is a weekly that gives me some inputs from the fantasyland of Washington.

Perhaps the leading edge of thinking in this country is that reflected in *Commentary,* published by the American Jewish Committee. At this point in its history, it is a centrist journal, full of very well informed and responsible material on the direction of America and the world.

I am invariably shocked when I ask people in my own organization, "What about so-and-so?" referring to something in the morning paper, and they don't know anything about it. After all, many of the people they meet will be aware of what is happening in the world, and so should they.

An executive in particular has a responsibility to be aware of contemporary events. Often, things that happen in one part of the world or in one part of the country will eventually become movements that some day might affect the executive. For example, early in 1965 I read a book called *New York Riots 1964,* written by two newsmen. I thought, "We are going to have one of those here," because I had noticed the happenings in other places. On August 11, 1965, the riots started in Los Angeles, and as they began, they developed just like the New York riots. Violence started that night, went up to a certain level, and then stopped, in the middle of the night. The next night, violence went up a little higher and then stopped again. I talked to Bill Parker, then chief of police, and told him that I thought we were going to have to fill the jails with rioters. I just did not believe that the then-popular theory of backing off would work. He followed my suggestion, for the first and only time. He didn't normally like my suggestions, but that night he put Deputy Chief Tom Reddin and me out as the field command staff.

Those riots in Los Angeles went almost according to the pattern of the riots in New York City and other urban riots. If the police wait until disaster or tragedy strikes to start responding to it, they are going to do a pretty poor job. If they are aware of contemporary events and anticipate things, they can quickly take care of changing situations, particularly emergencies, much more effectively. When a tragedy or national disaster hits suddenly, like a ton of bricks, it is no time to ask to be briefed on the reasons why it happened.

With awareness comes a certain level of confidence. That awareness involves a great deal, including a feel for—or better still, an understanding of—the human and cultural environment in which a leader must work. It includes knowing both the people whom the leader serves and the people who work for him. Cultivating that awareness and an education to go with it are pivotal elements in the development of potential leaders.

COMMUNITY AWARENESS

Before a community in America can effectively be served, a basic fact must be understood—that each community is unique. There are no two communities that are exactly alike, just as there are no two human beings exactly alike. Each one of us is different from any one of the billions of people who have been born on the face of the earth. Just look around, and you will see that no two people are exactly alike. Even identical twins, who may fool us on rare occasions, are not truly identical. If people are that different, then communities are certainly different. The people of Los Angeles are totally different from the people in San Diego. And as the distance between places increases, the differences grow. An understanding of the people who make up a community, and of their culture, including the history of that culture, is absolutely vital.

The Ethnic Makeup of the Community

If some energetic student would complete a Master's thesis, or if someone would write a book on a particular city—Los Angeles, Honolulu, whatever—for the sole purpose of identifying and describing the various cultural mixes within it in terms of the problems that police should be perceptive of, that person would make a significant contribution to public peace. Such a work would be a tremendous resource to police professionals. Besides being a very useful tool for a great many special community programs, it would assist the police leader with personnel decisions within his agency.

For example, over 60 years ago, hundreds of thousands of Armenians died at the hands of their Turkish conquerors, and to this day there is tremendous hostility toward the Turks by the Armenians. Not too long ago, a murder occurred in Santa Barbara, California, because of that hostility over the 60-year-old massacre. From a policing standpoint, it is a very sensitive thing when there are organized meetings of Americans of Turkish and Armenian descent at the same time and the same place. The Croatians and the Serbs have a similar problem. Many people in our harbor area of San Pedro are of Serbian and Croatian origins; they are ready to go to war at any time over things that happened back in the old country, possibly decades and even hundreds of years ago. Being sensitive to those conditions and understanding them are extremely important leadership traits.

Recently, Los Angeles has experienced a growth in the number of Koreans settling in our city. We had a Korean population of about 8,000 ten years ago; by 1975, that population had increased to 80,000, and it is still growing very rapidly. We found that a number of our Korean people were being victimized by other ethnic groups but were not reporting these crimes. Because my people could see the problem, liaison was established with the leaders of the Korean community, and they were asked to come in and talk to us about the problem of victimization. We learned from them about a special tension among themselves that my department had not know of before. There were two factions within our Korean community; one identified with the government of South Korea, and the other was an anti-Park force. The two groups were strongly at odds with one another even though they were now in America and shared many of the same problems. We try to understand these conditions; we believe it is important to be sensitive to these differences without taking sides.

One faction whose representatives came in had its own photographer, and they wanted him to take a picture of the leader of that group shaking his finger at me. The photograph would indicate that the Korean leader was telling the chief of police to protect the Korean community, and it would be published in all the Korean papers. I let them take the picture, because I knew it was important to that community. It would combat the belief by some of their people that they were not being accepted by the established community.

There are tremendous mixes of cultures in most parts of the United States of America, and there are always tremendous hidden problems; and yet the police, particularly when things change rapidly, are not always perceptive of them. The Asian community historically has not taken its problems to the police. Within our own old and well-established Japanese community, people suffer in silence or avenge themselves privately. The young Chinese gangs, the Wah Ching and others, some of them from Hong Kong, have viciously victimized older, established residents in Chinatown, in both San Francisco and Los Angeles, even to the extent of murder and extortion. The Koreans have some of that same thing.

Thus, very recently, we created an Asian Task Force. Some day, somebody will make a television series about this interesting group, as they did with SWAT. The Asian squad is really fantastic. There are about eight guys, and they are kept so busy with the community's problems that they are almost submerged into the Asian community. We will probably have to increase the size of the squad, but because of them, we are already beginning to serve the Asian community much better.

We also have a tremendous number of illegal entrants from Mexico, and they are also victimized, often by Mexican-Americans who understand the culture better and who use the language to cheat them out of fantastic sums of money.

Far too often, they are cheated out of all they own, particularly by scams that claim they will get the entrant's parents or family into the country legally. The poor entrant loses hundreds of dollars to the con artist. But the guy is here illegally, and he is not about to go to the police station to complain.

To help solve this problem, we put some Spanish-speaking officers in an old, dilapidated storefront on the east side of Los Angeles, calling it *Operacion Estafadores,* which means "Operation Swindler." Normally, illegal entrants will not go where there are symbols of authority, and yet here, they came streaming in. The entrant can go to this storefront, talk to a plainclothes Mexican or Spanish-speaking officer, and make a complaint. There is a tremendous need for this kind of police service. Without it, there may result a lowering of the quality of life for those people. If there is a lack of understanding about the culture and the intricacies of the people being served, they simply cannot be served. It is a frequent police problem everywhere, and it is one that seldom receives the attention it deserves.

Understanding the Jewish culture is another excellent example. For instance, Hasidic Jews are quite different from most other Jewish people. In New York, where there are a great many Hasidic Jews, if a police car comes into their neighborhood, they will surround it. They are not threatening the policemen; that is just the way they act. They just like to get on top of things. That is their way. New York policemen have to be trained to realize that these people are their friends; they are, in fact, very supportive. If another group surrounded that same car, it might be an altogether different story. It has to be remembered that these Jews believe that where a law is involved, it should be enforced right to the letter. When I walk into an affair where there are these Hasidim, I feel like a left-wing radical or something; they believe so firmly in the Bible, the Old Testament, and they believe in obeying the law so strongly that they get very exercised about the subject. So a tremendous difference does exist even within many cultures, and understanding those differences is absolutely vital to being able to get a particular community to open up and cooperate with the police.

If the police are going to get the job done with public cooperation, they must know the people they are trying to get cooperation from. If they are going to get reports of problems from such an area, they are going to have to have channels of communication open to that community. That is really where the so-called community-relations problem lies. It is a question of understanding the tremendous cultural and ethnic differences as they should be understood to properly serve the people from a police standpoint. It has always been interesting to me that these problems are so poorly understood.

The perfect solution would seem to be having every person entering a new land cast off his former culture completely. But of course, it will never be that simple, and besides, it would not be good for America. Instead, we must cultivate an understanding of each other's cultures. A young Japanese police officer, for example, must understand how Koreans feel about the Japanese, or he will not be able to interpret the feelings and actions of Koreans properly. Koreans generally feel very oppressed. They feel that they are a type of slave labor, and in many cases they have been. Long ago they were conquered and subjugated by the Japanese, and you will find some strong feelings between the Koreans and the Japanese. The Japanese-American policeman must know and understand this.

There is another way to look at it. There might very well be something we do as Americans that is legal and proper here, but that is a violation of some law or ethical percept in Japan or Korea. Likewise, there might be some act that is legal in Korea and improper here. It is important that police officers understand this, because it might help them do a better job and it might help them with routine decisions.

Now, if a Korean lived in Japan, he would probably live in a little community of nobody else but Koreans. This would put him as far away as possible from the mainstream of the Japanese community. He might be part of a culture group designed to protect the foreign part of his culture. That little group might at some time become victimized by Japanese criminals. If the Japanese police came into his community to find out how this Korean and his neighbors were doing and tried to learn of their cultural differences, those Koreans would think that the police were really giving proper service. It would be wrong to expect those people to abandon their culture. Their culture is what keeps them together, and it is unthinkable to require them to be homogenized, like milk.

It is unthinkable, in fact, that people should be homogenized in any terms. I am English, Irish, and Welsh and proud of that heritage. I know very keenly how the English look upon the Irish and the Welsh parts of me. During a recent trip I made to London, however, they tolerated me because there was enough English in me. Instead of Polish jokes, they tell Irish jokes there. The Irishman in England is the low man on the totem pole. After I gave a speech in London in 1975, I was praised by Lord Walston. I said, "Well, I've got the gift for gab of an Irishman, the acting ability of a Welshman, and the brain of an Englishman, so I *should* be able to give a good speech." He said, "Ah, but suppose you had the brain of an Irishman?"

Some immigrants may adhere to a custom of their country that involves a violation of our local law. A problem like that should be worked out with that community. That does not mean that we excuse the violation. If a law states, for example, that people are not supposed to carry knives, then the law should be explained to people whose native custom is to carry a knife. That is a police function. But if the police are not communicating with those people, the message cannot get across. It is a cultural thing. The police must be able to say, "You have to change part of your culture, because that breaks the law, and we are not going to overlook that just because you have cultural differences." Illegal customs have to be abandoned, but if we are not communicating with those people, they will not know the law. Maybe the kids of such an immigrant would keep their father from having a knife illegally if the police had a "basic-car" meeting in that neighborhood and discussed that cultural problem. It certainly would be better than having no communication with them until one of them pulled his knife on another person.

The great advantage of the basic-car type of meeting or the neighborhood-watch type of meeting, which will be discussed in greater detail later, is that they enable the policemen themselves to learn these cultural things on their own—things that they would never have known otherwise. In some of the Mexican areas, which were predominantly occupied by illegal aliens, my men learned, by meeting with the aliens and speaking in Spanish, that the parents were not sending their children to school. They were frightened that if they sent them to school, the family's presence would be discovered and they would be deported. Well, my officers made arrangements with the board of education in the area that there would be no reporting. These little Mexican kids were able to go to school, and it kept them off the streets; it helped to keep them from becoming burglars or some other type of criminals, and this worked to our advantage.

Awareness Through the Basic-Car Plan

In November 1969, we implemented a concept of community mobilization with a limited form of team policing called the Basic-Car Plan. The objective of the plan was to help society prevent crime by improving community attitudes toward the police, providing stability of assignment in the deployment of street policemen, and instilling in each team of officers a proprietary interest in their assigned area and a better knowledge of the police role in the community.

In Los Angeles, the city is divided into 17 *policing divisions*. Each of the divisions is further divided into areas called *reporting districts*. A reporting district is an area of a division having certain predetermined characteristics—in regard to population, size, type of structures, reported crime, and other factors as defined by the department's patrol formula.

Under the Basic-Car Plan, several reporting districts were assigned to a particular car. The number of districts assigned to any one car depended upon an analysis of the local problems in that area. Because of this, some of the policing divisions had seven or more basic cars, while others had four. Each basic-car team was composed of nine officers who provided 24-hour service to a particular area. A team was headed by a senior lead officer, a Policeman III + 1, and five senior policemen, Policeman III's. The remainder of the team was composed of Policeman II's and/or Policeman I's, trainees. Formal meetings were held with team members and citizens on a monthly basis, generally at a local school or other community building. This policing system was actually a prelude to full team policing.

In June 1972, the department began its first comprehensive experiment in total team policing. Under team policing, several basic cars and supportive services were reorganized under the supervision of a lieutenant, a team leader. The number of personnel assigned to each team leader varies according to the workload and crime of a specific area. The team leader is like a chief of police of a small district in the city. He is responsible for all police activities in that area, and he is held accountable for the results of his effort.

We have many meetings where no English is spoken. We give bilingual pay bonuses for Japanese, Chinese, anything we need. In all those areas, we give a 2½ percent pay bonus for the ability to use the foreign language colloquially, and a 5½ percent pay bonus if it can be used both colloquially and through the formal written word.

Yet there are some problems. For example, a really fine Japanese-American recruit was asked how his Japanese was, and he told us that he was raised in New York City and did not know one word of Japanese. Many officers with Spanish surnames have lost their knowledge of the Spanish language

69

or have never acquired it. This can create a problem on the street for the officer, because when people see his name, they immediately jump to the conclusion that he can speak their language. If he cannot, they believe he has a status problem.

COMMUNITY LEADERS

Some people believe that all problems can be readily resolved through so-called community leaders, rather than by making that vital contact with the community itself. My own department went through the process of trying to work with community leaders, principally in the black neighborhoods. We discovered a very serious problem with that approach—namely, who appoints community leaders? No one! They are very often self-anointed and self-appointed people, frequently involved in an attempt to exploit their own people. The guy who says, for example, "I am the head black man down in this district, so come and see me," is generally not the real leader. He may have some of the politicians catering to him, and eventually, if he has, he will get some type of federal grant siphoned through him so he can apply his methods to resolve some community problem. It generally sounds like a good idea. His own success is almost assured. But far too often, those efforts mean only problems for everyone, especially those who must still live in the community and live with the program. We tried going that route with so-called community leaders, and our efforts failed.

From my own painful experiences, I know why trying to work out problems through community leaders does not work in black areas—or white areas, for that matter, or almost any other kind of area. Ask youself, how many people have a non-elected representative of their community who can clearly speak for them on all community problems? Most people in most communities do not have such a leader who is capable of speaking for them. These so-called community leaders are "professionals" at their business—professional blacks, professional Mexicans, professional Chinese, whatever. They make their living claiming to be leaders of a small community of interest. When officialdom caters to these leaders, they acquire tremendous power over other people's lives without the benefit of any type of election, and they can become oppressive tyrants.

We should refuse to be limited to dealing with only the select few who consider themselves to be community leaders. There are some true, indigenous leaders within a community, and they are great. But you have to be able to tell the truly great ones from the phony ones. It isn't really that difficult, because the true leader will be obvious. He will be the one who still lives in the community and who is putting his community's interest ahead of his own. Such people are easy to spot because there are so few of them.

Occasionally I will sit and talk to community leaders, but I also go around them and talk to others. The ability to go around them is an important point, because a government official can get trapped by having some guy saying that he is the leader of the area, only to find later that he is really just one source of input. That is a very real danger. It is at that point that some leaders start to think of themselves as some kind of godfather. Godfathers do some good things for people, but most often they extract an awful price for their service.

8

Police Leadership
and Agency Personnel

KNOWING AND UNDERSTANDING
YOUR PEOPLE

While understanding and knowing the community is important, it is perhaps equally important to the successful leader to
know and understand the people he leads, the people within
the organization. This means knowing how they feel, and
how they think, and what they are concerned about. First and
foremost, a leader must know the primary people doing the
basic job. The people in supporting roles who work in various
other, less basic functions must also be known, as well as
others in the hierarchy. But the basic people are the most
important.

How does a leader get to know his own men? One thing that will *not* provide this knowledge is a belief that his own experience will serve as the best source of information. A leader is of higher rank, and most of his experience is both outdated and outmoded. It is virtually useless to refer to one's own experience in order to understand how subordinates feel in today's world. A leader has to relate to the here and now of people's feelings; the world that once was is of limited value. There are two methods to accomplish this quest for knowledge that have been very useful to me.

The first one is to meet in a planned program on a regular basis with the people down at the bottom of the organization and listen to them. For example, every month a different group of men is brought in for retraining at the Police Academy. Once a month, my assistant chiefs and I get together for two hours and listen to the people in the rank of policeman. We go around the room and tell them, "Here is your chance to straighten out the police department. If we're doing anything wrong, if there's something you need that you're not getting and that we can give you, if there is something we should be doing, here is your chance to straighten us out." And they know we mean it. They open up and tell us all kinds of things.

The second step in that process deals with another group of my policemen, those with a higher classification, my senior policemen. A different group of them visits with me every month for coffee. My three assistant chiefs are with me at this meeting, but no one else. We start the meeting by telling those men that they are chiefs of police of little districts of the city; if there is anything the brass are doing that is making it difficult for them to do their job, or if there is anything that can be done to make it easier or make them more effective, this is their chance. I tell them I have the three assistant chiefs, my "troika," and if we have made a bad policy we have the right people to change it right there. And we go around the room for answers.

Today, policemen speak out. It was different when I was

a policeman. Back then, we would not have spoken out, we would have just dummied up. But beginning as far back as the end of World War II, the young men coming back from the military started to have more individualistic feelings. Policemen would come to the brass and tell them something. My policemen are very outspoken with me and with the rest of the brass. They speak out when there is a problem, and that is when we need them the most.

The three assistant chiefs and I sit there and learn a great deal about our city and about the men. At a meeting in the summer of 1975, we learned that there was a group of white, English-speaking people who were alienated from society because of their poverty. They were being victimized and not reporting crime. And the men taught us something about the elderly Jewish people who were living in the Fairfax area of Hollywood—people who still had serial numbers tattooed on their arms from being prisoners in Nazi Germany, readied to go to the gas chambers. The officers told us all about these people, what they were afraid of and what the police had done to help them—and more important, what *we* could do, as members of the brass, to help them. We would never have known about some of the terrorism that was going on in this well-established Jewish community except through my men.

Many of those people were so old that they would get lost and nobody could figure out who they were. So the officers started a big status thing: They went to the Department of Motor Vehicles and they got non-driver identification cards for these old people. This was a nice sort of a status thing. The policemen had figured out a relatively easy way to help those people and at the same time make themselves more effective and their jobs easier.

Frequently I find at these meetings that there has been a total failure to get information down the chain of command. It might have got down to a certain level, but no further. The meeting gives me a method of getting my message across and correcting a problem at the same time.

These kinds of meetings with policemen provide tremendous two-way communication. There are many things they want that are impractical, of course. For example, they want longer hair, or they may want to get rid of their hats because the cost of hair spray is so high. We did modify the hair standards slightly so that they could wear their hair a little longer, but we said to hell with the hair spray when it came to not wearing the hat. We were not going to have the men or women wearing their hair so long that it impaired the proper wearing of the uniform cap. When they got out on the street at night on foot, we didn't want some other policeman shooting at them in the belief that they might be suspects. We also wanted the public to know who the officers were, so they wouldn't be shooting at them either. We want a uniform and cap that stands out as a distinctive marking or symbol.

But at least I know now how they feel about caps and how they feel about hair. And they know where I stand. That is important. We've given them a little bit more hair than they had before, although some of them are now losing it. They know that I am flexible to a degree. But they also know as a result of such meetings that there are limits, and they know the reasons for those limits.

Another meeting I have regularly is with the whole range of working-level people, including supervisors and middle managers. Besides the lower levels, it includes Policemen III + 1, senior policemen from basic cars; sergeants from different teams; investigators, also from different teams; and lieutenants. Each of the sixteen participants is from a different district. This meeting is extremely effective because it involves the four lowest ranks of the department. A policeman may say that his lieutenant is doing a great job, but that the other lieutenants in the division are not doing much of anything. Or perhaps he wants to complain about his lieutenant's policies, and one of the other lieutenants in this meeting might be able to help him find a solution to his problem. Having them from different districts helps a great deal.

At one point, we used to have captains at those meetings; but a policeman once said, right in front of his captain, "You've asked me a question, but you shouldn't expect me to answer it straight, because my own captain is sitting up at the end of the table. I want to complain about the way he's running his division, and I'm going to do it in spite of the fact that you have him here. I am going to do that because I think he's really screwing it up." Finally, he suggested that in the future, captains should not be there. I took his suggestion, and since then I have only had the four working ranks and my three assistants present. The main reason I have my three assistants with me is to educate them on staying in touch with the bottom of the organization.

That pretty much takes care of the contact with people up through the rank of lieutenant, other than actual working situations, which are the worst time to try to make corrections or small talk. Police people in particular resent a boss who is around when something is going wrong and wants to make some change right on the spot. The work is too important to do that.

We have another meeting that includes the other levels in the department. These are what I call vertical staff meetings; they include five levels of authority: the chief of police, one of the three assistant chiefs, one of the bureau deputy chiefs, two commanders who have specialized responsibilities, and each of the captains in this same chain of command.

Under team policing, of course, we have some captains who are responsible for everything, but we still have some who are responsible for special investigations. You can look at the five captains in the meeting, for example, and tell them this is their chance to straighten things out. You tell them, if they think things are screwed up in this department, tell us about it. Do you have any problems? If you have a problem, it can be resolved very easily by one of the chiefs here. One captain might look at his watch and say, "You got enough time? You think we've got problems, but you probably don't have enough time to match the problems we've got." The captain will talk about this or that problem. I think out loud, "My God, we solved that one a year ago. Didn't we say we were going to do so-and-so?" I look around at the responsible assistant chief and ask, "What about that?" Usually he will say, "I don't know why they don't know about that," and then he will turn to the deputy chief next to him and ask the same thing. I can guarantee that communication broke down. Communication was just lost.

I have a principle—we call it Davis's Law—that says communication cannot traverse more than two levels in a hierarchy accurately, in either direction, up or down. I defy anyone to show me any kind of an order that travels more than two levels in the hierarchy accurately and effectively— which means that it is not questioned and that everyone understands what it means. That just cannot happen. Most communication is dysfunctional in the light of what it is supposed to accomplish. A simple memo can be read by several different people and interpreted several different ways. Even legal statutes are subject to this same problem. Laws are written by lawyers; they must be interpreted by lawyers, and lawyers often have to decide what the laws say. Even then, it is infrequent indeed that all the lawyers will agree. Organizational communication is much like the law, and the people interpreting it are much like society's lawyers.

Thus, the meetings described here are extremely effective. Everyone there, on all four or five levels, is hearing the same thing at the same time. Perhaps the assistant chief has been reporting that everything is rosy, but we find out that it is all screwed up. It might involve some policy that we had worked out, or thought we had worked out, with the district attorney's office on the filing of felony complaints. But now we find that it is not working out the way that everyone had agreed it was going to work. So we start over again, hoping that this time we find a real solution.

I spend a great deal of my time doing these internal things within the department. My whole day is spent running the police department. I try to make it a point never to give a luncheon speech. I'll occasionally make personal appearances at night, but only on rare occasions do I give a speech at noon, because I want to spend my time listening to my people—not talking to them, but listening to them. If I talk to them, I'm not learning a damn thing, and they are probably learning very little themselves because their minds are on something they think is really a problem. When I'm talking about some internal difficulty, they couldn't care less about it, because they have a problem they want to discuss. So I listen.

So the effective leader must know the people in the community and he must know his men, and he must know how they feel *today,* not how they felt when he was one of them, five, ten, or twenty years ago. Things change so rapidly that the leader has to be right on top of them, right now. Is that generally done in most police departments regularly? Are sergeants always listening to their men? Do all lieutenants and all captains listen? It's amazing what a leader can learn.

There is no loss of ego involved when a leader doesn't know the solution to some problem. I get stumped all the time; I don't know all the answers. Most people probably believe I am no smarter than they are. In fact, many may think I am sort of a dummy. It doesn't really bother me when I get stumped on a problem and cannot come up with some wonderful magic solution. Sometimes, as people move up the ladder, they tend to become rather pompous and think that everyone believes they're brilliant. Well, most high-ranking leaders are not really any smarter or any dumber than their subordinates. They just have a different perspective and a different set of responsibilities.

There has been a great deal of information published on the subject of individual and group perceptions. This is often referred to as group dynamics.[1] For example, there are three kinds of people in any group when you conduct a

[1]S.E. Seashore, *Group Cohesiveness in the Industrial Group* (Ann Arbor, Mich.: Institute of Social Research, 1955).

conference. There are those who are brand new to the group. Let's say it is their first day on the job, and they are aware that everyone knows they are new. Because of their generally acknowledged ignorance of the particular subject matter, they are not ashamed to ask questions. That kind of person will say, "I never heard that term before; what does it mean?" Someone explains to him what it means. Everyone realizes that he wasn't necessarily supposed to know the answer, and he didn't lose face in asking.

Next, there are those that are paid to know. They are supposed to know certain things and they have a lot to lose. They are not going to ask questions. If they don't know the answer, they are going to keep their mouths shut, because they are paid to know.

Then there are those people in the meeting who know everything there is to know about the subject. They are the distinguished experts; because of their status, they don't have to show off, and they are going to just sit there being very quiet, unless you call on them. If you do call on them, they will impart a little wisdom.

The first guy, the guy who is new, isn't supposed to know anything, and he will be willing to put his hand up and ask questions, but not the guy in the middle. Not the guy who is supposed to know and is getting paid for it, but is a fake. He is never going to acknowledge his ignorance by asking a question on something he is supposed to know. In dealing with these kinds of meetings you have to be aware of this phenomenon and exercise caution by not embarrassing people.[2] We have been fortunate in and absolutely gratified by the willingness of my subordinates to come right out and put it on the line.

There are certain kinds of meetings we *don't* have. We don't have great big staff meetings of deputy chiefs and great

[2]K. Lewin, "Studies in Group Decision," in *Group Dynamics: Research and Theory,* eds. D. Cartwright and A. Zander (Evanston, Ill.: Row, Peterson, 1953).

big staff meetings of captains and great big staff meetings of commanders, because we have found that they are an absolute waste of time. I played that game for two years. Because we had only weekly assistant chiefs' meetings, some people believed that I was isolated and did not really know what was happening. They would say, "If only he would listen to us, then he would really know." So I started having big staff meetings with deputy chiefs and with my commanders. The night before a meeting, I would hear one of them saying, "Boy, if he would only listen to me, I would really tell him how it is." When I went to the meeting, I would call on that man who was supposedly ready to tell me about all these problems. I would say, "Mac, how are things going?"

"Oh, just great, chief, just great. No problems at all."

"Everything is just going great?" I would retort. "And there are no problems?"

Quickly he would reply, "No, chief, you're doing a great job, chief."

Then I would go around the room, and not one of these guys would come up with anything. They were all beating their gums saying that I needed to have them in a weekly staff meeting so they could keep me from being dumb. I might have needed that—in fact, I probably do—but they didn't do the job of making me smart.

People think that just because they are paid to know what's going on, they automatically possess knowledge. In my department, I would learn absolutely nothing from them. Why? Because they don't know very much. Things go up only two levels from them; they might know what captains tell them and they might even know what lieutenants tell them, but nothing that the sergeant ever says gets up to them, and nothing that the chief ever says gets down through them. We have wasted all kinds of time with my commanders in commanders' meetings but no more.

One time, Pat Murphy said to me, "You know, when I was commissioner of New York, I used to ask my inspectors how the men felt about something."

I said, "Pat, don't you realize not that your inspectors probably tried to help you, but they didn't know how your men felt, because they were inspectors. They weren't men. They were inspectors."

That fact regarding the hierarchical levels and how they are insulated from information both up and down is very important.[3] A leader can't run an organization founded on a scalar structure and try to communicate down through it. He has to use shortcuts, such as meeting with working-level people and listening to them. We conduct vertical staff meetings with five ranks present to get the brass input, instead of horizontal meetings with all one rank. The result is absolutely tremendous; I learn things I would never know otherwise. I would have been out of business by now if I had not developed those techniques.

ETHNIC BALANCE

If police work is going to be done in cooperation with the people in the community, it is going to be necessary that everyone in that community feel some identification with the police agency. If there is a pretty good percentage of Hawaiians in the community but there are no Hawaiian policemen in the department, then the public is going to feel less comfortable with its police department. A police agency, theoretically, should approximate the ethnic composition of the community to properly relate to the community. I say "theoretically," because good policemen come in all colors, and the pigmentation of skin should not be the overriding factor in good police service. Yet common sense would dictate some desire for achieving an ethnic balance. The achievement of an ethnic balance serves also to give reality to the previously discussed

[3]Lewin, "Studies in Group Decisions," p. 144.

subject of knowing and understanding the community we serve.[4]

Now, does this ideal of achieving an ethnic balance mean that we should lower hiring standards for certain ethnic groups in order to get a ratio of those groups in the police department? The answer across the country is frequently yes, and sometimes by virtue of a court order. The courts have said that many police departments must maintain a minority list and a majority list—the majority, of course, being white, and minorities being any other ethnic groups, usually blacks and Latin Americans. For years Denver had to take one candidate from the minority list and one from the white list. Also, some cities are now under court orders requiring them to take one female and one male until they get to a certain mixture of the sexes.

Does this mean that the person on the minority list isn't qualified? Not necessarily. It means that of several people who took the same examination, some are being selected differently because of race or sex. The person on the minority list might be number 100 on an integrated list, but on the mandated list of selection, he or she might be number 15. It means that everyone is qualified at some point, but that the selection will not be of the relatively more qualified people in the group. That kind of arrangement is not very healthy for either the employing agency or the taxpayers.

Instead, we should look inside organizations for ways of attempting to reflect the ethnicity of the community and achieving it fairly for everyone. Probably the best solution to the recruitment problem is selective recruiting. Everyone would have to qualify, but by means of specialized recruiting on a positive basis, there would be less chance for an inequity occurring. In Los Angeles, we have a real problem getting a

[4]National Advisory Commission on Criminal Justice Standards and Goals, *Police* (Washington, D.C.: U.S. Government Printing Office, 1973).

representation of blacks, Mexican-Americans, and Asians. Many Asian parents, for instance, want their kids to be doctors and lawyers and teachers and professors, not policemen. My department has been actively seeking minority candidates, and we have established a regular Recruitment Division. It is headed by a captain who happens to be black, and contains everything in the rainbow in terms of ethnicity. We also have female recruiters. What has to be done is to selectively find minority candidates who have the education, the background, the interest, and the other required qualifications to be police officers. We try to talk them into being Los Angeles police officers, and in doing so, we come closer to bringing the community and the police together.

Achieving an ethnicity within a police force is not just something that you have to do to comply with the Fair Employment Practices laws. Human beings, generally, are sufficiently protective of their own ethnicity. Most ethnic groups look upon themselves as being a little bit better, a little superior, and there is a great inclination to just tune other groups out. Some people even say, "I do not want anyone but this kind of people to work with me, because they and I are a little bit better." However, if you do not seek to achieve some common denominator with the ethnicity of your community, you are not going to have personnel who will be accepted totally by the whole community.

A community should at least have police officers who fully understand cultural differences. It has been amply demonstrated that human beings, properly educated and trained, are about equally capable of doing almost anything. For that reason, ethnicity should be sought as an organizational objective. Such objectives should preclude the necessity for judicial mandates. When those mandates become necessary in the minds of those in power, it is already too late. Remedial efforts will work only when they are genuinely undertaken by an individual community that has recognized the need for such a balance.

The internalized process needed for this understanding

of ethnicity is not something that can be mandated by bureaucratic or judicial rule. As with many factors involving human nature, it must come from the heart. Unfortunately, rules of law and mandates of most bureaucrats are far too often inadequate in achieving goals of the heart. In fact, they often hamper what might normally be achieved without interference. They appear to stir up the latent bias and bigotry that might normally remain hidden and uninfluential. Not all of society's ills can be resolved by rules of the mind—especially when ills of the heart are being discussed.

9

The Traits
of Police Leadership

Up to this point I have discussed some matters having to do with being a leader. Now I will deal specifically with the particular traits important to leadership. However, what I mean to discuss here are not those subjects the average reader might expect.

The standard traits of leadership have been discussed quite adequately in any number of texts and other books. There are some generally accepted characteristics we recognize in our leaders, and when they are compiled, you can count on a hybrid cross between a Boy Scout, a Presbyterian minister, and the president of the local PTA. Besides, it is my own view that an author should never try to cover the whole field with a subject like this. He should stick to what he believes in most strongly. In effect, he should pass on those "secrets" that have meant something to him. In my case, they have contributed to whatever success I have had.

COURAGE

Knowing Right from Wrong

Every good leader must possess courage; to phrase it more simply, he must have guts. Most of us know the difference between right and wrong. Our gut instinct tells us that one thing is right and another is wrong. The total of all our perceptions and that thing called conscience say, "This is right," or, "This is wrong." So when we come to a fork in the road, we generally know which way we should go.

But sometimes, doing the right thing is painful or hazardous or difficult; and when someone is leading other people, he is expected, because of his position, to take the outfit down the proper fork in the road. He must have the courage to go that way regardless of personal consequences. That is what having guts is all about—doing the right thing regardless of how much pain or difficulty it brings.

The antithesis would be for the leader to perceive the right way but, since it is painful, to select the other way simply because it is easier. Going the other way is going the wrong way, and it means pulling your people down with you. The wrong way will eventually eliminate any confidence and respect subordinates have in their leader. The temporary response may be one of support, since followers sometimes fear tough decisions as well, but in the end, their distrust will be manifested.

Many of the decisions that should be made by leaders are simply not made because they are too tough. The Watergate revelations of the early seventies, as an example, reflected this fairly clearly. There was just an absolute and total lack of courage and reverence for the law during Watergate. Even with all those lawyers, there was an absence of respect for the law. It was incredible! Many of the president's men, even though they certainly used the law, apparently did not believe in its sacredness. And then, those who did, those who might have changed the course of history, those who probably had pangs of conscience and the ability to say, "Hey, we can't do this," decided to follow their leaders down the wrong road. Nobody had the guts—despite any possible pangs of conscience—to say, "Wait a minute! The hell we are! We are not going to go that way. We are going to go the right way."

Not one man in that whole outfit had the guts to call the signals right. Some of them got there by the back door, but it took a congressional subpoena to do it. Others hid their courage in the anonymity of the press. I knew some of those men. I personally met with Egil Krogh, a very nice young man. He impressed me as a sort of Boy Scout type of lawyer. The reader will recall that he was the clean-cut fellow who admitted that he was wrong and that he was blaming no one.

It is still absolutely amazing to me that none of those leaders, our leaders, had the guts to say, "We made a mistake yesterday; we're not going to go any deeper." It is even more alarming that none of them had the guts to prevent the mistake from happening in the first place. Why did this thing happen? Why didn't someone have the guts to stop it?

Group Pressures

There is another aspect to having the guts to take the right road. It involves one of the strongest forces that comes to play on a human being. It is a product not of the individual's own mind, but of the concerted pressure of the group in which he dearly and sometimes desperately wants to be accepted. It involves that phenomenon called group dynamics, and the power of that force makes each one of us a different man when we are a part of a group.[1]

An example from the police world might be appropriate. A lieutenant with 50 men under him might privately ask an individual officer, "How do you think we ought to do such and such? Do you think we ought to try it this way?" The officer will think it over and say, "Yes, I think we should try it that way." The lieutenant's suggestion is the "right" thing to do. It may be a new way or it may even be a difficult way, but it is the right way. But if the lieutenant asks the same question of that man in front of the other 49 men, it is a different decision, perhaps even an unpopular decision. The officer, instead of saying, "Yes, I think we ought to do such-and-such," may say, "Well, there are a lot of things to consider in a situation such as this. There is a little problem here or there. I'm not sure that we want to change what we have been doing. I think, lieutenant, that I for one would not want to go down that road."

There is a decided difference now. It is the pressure of the group. That officer is thinking of the approbation of his peers, and it is a natural reaction. Group pressure is stronger on the member of a group than any leader's influence is. And when you can get the group to go along, then you've got a very powerful force to move something forward. If that lieutenant can figure out who the group leaders are, and if he can get them sold one by one and if he can get them committed to supporting an idea in front of the group, he can win the whole group at once. All it takes to undermine that lieutenant is one indigenous leader sitting in front of the room. When he says, "I think it would be a good idea if we did this instead,

[1] Eric Berne, *What Did You Say After You Said Hello?* (New York: Grove Press, 1976).

what do you think?'' and another guy who really respects him throws in his support, pretty soon a few others fall in line. By that time, the lieutenant is dead. That guy was stronger than the lieutenant. It happens time and time again.

But having the guts to do something means being willing to be lonesome, temporarily at least, because the courageous leader may not be loved by the group. Let me tell you, there are not many leaders with guts. They are few and far between. And it is easy to say that people should have guts, that they should have the intestinal fortitude to make the right choices, but very few of us want to be lonely. That is what the courageous leader must face.

We are in an age where group decisions are common. Certainly no intelligent leader would ignore the talent available to him inside his organization. But that process does not take away the leader's responsibility to speak up. Think of the group pressure involved when nearly everyone believed that the world was flat. Somebody had to be the first to say, ''Hey, the world is not flat. It's round.'' The guy who made a courageous statement about the world being round was obviously going to be considered a nut, and he was going to be unpopular. But somebody had to eventually say that and believe it.

Speaking as an administrator, it would be nice to have a few more Pattons and a few less pussycats. Real leadership, leadership with the guts to do the right thing, makes a tremendous difference in any organization.

FORCEFULNESS AND PERSUASIVENESS

A law enforcement leader must be forceful and persuasive—qualities that are an extension of being courageous. The police are involved in a type of work where there are many conflicts. So many pressure groups exist, including politicians and political groups; economic forces, both business and labor; illegal groups, such as the organized crime syndicates, which apply their own kind of pressure; and, most recently, women's groups and homosexual groups. All those groups constantly move about trying to whipsaw a police department. They are like different winds blowing at the same time, each trying in its own way to push the police off course, in their own special direction. A leader must stand up and be forceful to withstand these winds, and he must be persuasive in presenting his case to those groups that would materially or obviously reduce the effectiveness of his organization. Because of the lack of due process and security, too few police leaders are willing to take the risk involved in being forceful and persuasive.

One of the major responsibilities of a leader is the making of decisions. Unfortunately, many people hit the top spot and still hardly ever make a decision. I can recall going in to bosses and giving them the arguments in favor of making a change, and getting nothing but a bland smile. I wouldn't know whether I had convinced them or not until some time later. But an organization cannot run without decisions being made, particularly at the top.

Most of the decisions that make a police organization go forward are made out on the street. A policeman has to be decisive. A policeman can't sit around and wait and debate: "Am I going to arrest this guy? Am I going to search him? What are my grounds?" He can't go to a law library and look it all up. If we expect our policemen to make sound, timely judgments, we certainly have to expect their leaders to make sound and timely judgments. We probably never have all the facts we would like to have to make a decision; we are never able to totally define the problem in all its most minute detail. But with experience, good practical judgment, ability, and courage, decisions can be made, and in a timely fashion. In many cases, problems are increased greatly or get out of hand because of a failure on the part of a leader to make timely decisions.

FLEXIBILITY

A leader must also be flexible. He can never become totally calcified in his opinions. That does not mean that a chief executive cannot be strong and uncompromising with those things that are related to legal and moral principles; but he must also be sure that the things he is uncompromising about *are* matters of principle, and not just new situations that require rethinking or some change. Ours is a fast-changing world, and police work, like all things in that world, must be adaptable to changing demands in order to be effective.

There is a tendency on the part of those involved in the promotional and selection process to choose people who reflect the opinions of present superiors. It is probably human nature. The candidates who are favored tend to be reissued editions of the senior figures who select them, rather than people who might go in the opposite direction from the thinking of the top brass. This is not to suggest disloyalty, or behavior that goes against policy. But there are people who can accomplish things in a different fashion while still remaining within policy.

If an organization selects people, especially for the management hierarchy, who tend to reflect the values and standards, even the dress mode, of the superiors who make the selection, a serious condition will result. That organization will lack the kind of flexibility needed to properly meet day-to-day problems.

It is pretty well established in behavioral science research that after age 35, it is very tough to change individual attitudes. Most attitudes are pretty firmly fixed by that age. Even with extensive, highly scientific, and competent psychological counseling, it is unlikely that we can really change attitudes. Attitudes are habits. They are how we look at things. We immediately interpret something in terms of our attitudes. They are like the colored filter we put before a camera that makes it see things in a certain fashion. Therefore, leaders must work hard at remaining flexible without bending from principle. It is only in this way that they can recognize the progress that can be made.

Police organizations have come some distance from the past, in both refining procedures and improving services, and similar skills must be applied to the future. If we are preserving the status quo, then we are probably ensuring the death of the organization.

There are at least two kinds of organizational leaders. There are what might be termed "maintenance men"—the people who come in and take office and preserve things, whether it is a captaincy or inspectorship in a police organization, or some other kind of "managementship" in various other types of organizations. They preserve what they find, just the way a museum keeper does. They do not change anything. In fact, they are frequently against change. People like this probably have a certain utility. At least you know what they are going to do; they are going to keep everything just the way it was. But if we were a nation of maintenance men, preserving the status quo, we would disappear into oblivion.

Then, there are the "builders." The builders look at how the job can be done better. They seek to learn how they can be better managers. It is the builders who improve upon the world. Sometimes a builder must also tear down as he builds. He must be flexible enough in his outlook to see what must be done to help make the organization healthy and better, and yet do so without compromising principles. The builders are absolutely vital to any healthy organization.

AWARENESS OF IGNORANCE

One thing I have learned, through years of experience in supervision and management as well as many years of teaching, is that what I don't know is so great that it could fill a whole library. If I have had any success, it may very well be because I realize that I don't know very much. If there is a body of knowledge in my world, particularly my police world, and even more particularly within my department, the people under me, in the aggregate, know infinitely more about it than I know. This is what a person must understand in order to be a good leader; the ability to acknowledge this fact can best be described as humility. To be an effective leader, you have to have some humility. (I've never been accused of having very much of it, but in view of my high regard for the ability of so many people in my organization who can do things better than I can, I must possess some.)

If a leader tries to be all things to all people, and if he believes he knows everything, or that nothing could go forward without his great expertise, then nothing will ever happen. Any man who believes that has never become smart enough to learn what it takes to manage whatever kind of business he is in.

The new sergeant or manager shouldn't feel bad about feeling dumb, because he *is* dumb—that is, in terms of not knowing everything, not in terms of not being good. All his subordinates are going to say, "Boy, is he dumb!" If they didn't, there would be something wrong. If he wasn't dumb, there would be something wrong with him, and if they didn't think he was dumb, there would be something wrong with them. It is absolutely unimportant to be that "great expert." He has to have some knowledge of the business, but the main thing he has to have knowledge about is himself. If he understands himself, he can understand those other human beings he works with. Understanding other people through understanding ourselves is probably one of the best ways of starting out on the road to being a good leader.

No one should be ashamed of this kind of ignorance. Each of us is ignorant about so many things. Few of us are highly knowledgeable in any given specialty, including police work. There is always at least one other person who knows much more than we do. A man may think he is the best vice or narcotic officer, or the best homicide investigator, but I guarantee that if you look around, you can find somebody better.

It is very important that people not cut themselves off from information by pretending to know everything. No one person is really that knowledgeable. There are a number of facts about America that President Carter does not know. There are many things about New York that its mayor does not know. It is the same with everyone. An effective leader cannot be afraid to say, "I do not know." That way, the people in his organization are enabled to teach him what he doesn't know without shocking his ego or making him feel insecure.

LISTENING ABILITY

Executives, particularly those at the top, must do a great deal of listening. Listening means more than just keeping your mouth shut. It means concentrating on what a person is saying, including looking at the expression on the person's face, and listening to the tone of his voice. It usually means being able to tune in, so that you can, by evaluation of the words, attitudes, looks, glances, and all other manifestations of the other person's attempted communication, perceive what he means and show it by feeding it back to him.

When a subordinate talks to a person of superior rank, it takes courage for him to come out and say some things, things that might be a little easier to say if the ranks were equal. The leader has to be willing to listen and closely evaluate what is being said. There is a technique called understanding listening. It is a method of not just hearing the words that a person says but trying to listen for and feel—actually seek out—what he is really trying to say. Most of us, even the most honest among us, tend to hold back a bit when we speak. We do not want the total extent of our feelings to be expressed, so we speak somewhat cautiously. Yet it is important for the boss to know as precisely as he can what a person means by what he is saying.

Understanding listening requires a sensitivity in regard to the words, the tone of voice, even what is *not* said, to determine what the speaker means by what he has said. It also requires some knowledge of the possible group influences on the speaker, if the conversation takes place in a meeting. Everything that is heard must be cross-evaluated with other inputs on the same subject. Only after what is said is compared can he properly evaluate the substance of the statement.

Occasionally a person who perceives a problem will come to the boss with what he thinks is the solution. Usually there are no specific solutions, there are only specific problems. Every problem is unique and specific. Problems, like people, are different and should not be generalized about. So in the process of understanding listening, the leader should attempt to define the problem. Solutions are relatively unimportant, because with an understanding of the dimensions of a specific problem, the solution or solutions are fairly easy to come by. The difficult task is a specific definition of the problem. Good listening will assist the problem solver in his ability to correctly judge a problem so that proper solutions can be discerned.

COURTESY

Policing, of all professions and occupations, by its very nature tends to make other people ill at ease. Because of his authority to arrest, and other people's knowledge of that authority, every policeman carries real power. Every person who commits some violation, perhaps only a failure to stop at a signal, is apprehensive of authority. In view of this fact, if the police are to gain the optimum amount of public cooperation, it is extremely important that a police agency be the most courteous agency of local government. Instead, by the very nature of the job and the harshness of the world that policemen rub up against, the police tend to become rather sour and cynical and cryptic in the way they talk to people.

The police usually answer the phone, "Robbery, Smith." No greeting. No explanation. No way for anyone but the initiated to know what the guy on the other end means. Now, when a citizen who has been robbed calls and Smith answers the phone, the victim might think that he would rather not deal with this man. Smith might sound even worse than the guy who stuck him up.

Sometime, when you have nothing better to do, call your own police agency and listen to how the phone is answered. It is pretty bad in most agencies. Generally you get the impression, "Drop dead." Six years ago, we directed our people to start every phone call with "Good morning," or "Good evening," or "Good afternoon," then the name of the division, the officer's name, and the words, "May I help you?" The change was resented and resisted at first, but it had to be accepted or I would have chopped off a few heads.

The whole idea started one day in a meeting with my top staff. I turned on the conference microphone and began dialing around the city. I let my staff officers listen to the way the public was being treated on the telephone. I asked them how they would like to be treated that way by cops. They squirmed. Obviously, they did not like it. So we made the change. Now, everyone in my department, almost without exception, says, for instance, "Good evening, Robbery Division, Sergeant Smith, may I help you?"

Some people objected to this kind of greeting because it took so long to say. Others, however, have told me that about halfway through, they begin to feel a little bit civilized. One officer said, "I got up one morning angry with my wife. I didn't touch breakfast, and I left the house angry. When I got to work, I got on that phone and said, "Good morning, Officer Smith, such and such a place." He said that by the time he had started to say, "May I help you?" he really felt like helping someone. He was not mad at the world any more.

Years ago, as a brand new policeman just out of the academy, I was working at Central Division. Central had an old desk man named Durkee. He was just plain nasty. He was nasty even to other policemen; a lot of the oldtimers were that way to the younger policemen. There was one day when Durkee had to give me something; I have forgotten what it was exactly. He was so abrupt and cryptic that he made me want to fight. I was about to take this old Durkee on when one of the sergeants got hold of me and said, "Hey, kid he's a real mean old man. You've got to watch that old man. He is tough and he has whipped more kids your age than you can poke a stick at. You had better go back up to the gym and do some more boxing if you are going to try to take Durkee on." I repressed my anger, but I soon found that I had started saying, "Davis!" over the phone, and for 29 years, even at the time when I made chief, I was still talking the same way over the telephone—and so was everyone else.

We have changed. Officers in my department have always been required, even back when I went through the academy in 1940, to say, when writing a traffic citation, "Good morning, may I see your operator's license?" The same guys that answered the phone so gruffly, if they were giving a ticket, would always say, "Good morning," because they were disciplined to say that. We certainly got more compliments on our ticket manners than we did on our telephone manners. People wrote letters and said that they did not appreciate getting the ticket, but that the officer's courtesy had made it easier. That has been going on for years now.

There is no need to be gruff or short or caustic in our dealing with people over the telephone, just as it doesn't pay to be that way in giving tickets. The police should always start with courtesy; when it is necessary to tell someone to "drop that gun, you no-good so-and-so," *then* whatever force is necessary to control that kind of person will be understood. If a policeman is going to arrest someone who is wanted for robbery and he knows that the man has a gun, the policeman will have a pretty good reason for getting behind that guy and knocking him on his face first before he talks to him. That's okay. That's good police work. There are times when the police can postpone the amenities. You knock the robber

99

down, and *then* you say, "Good morning, sir. I will now inform you of your rights." A very small percentage of police work is like that.

As a police leader, I don't want anyone to get hurt. The concept of courtesy involves the average John Doe who calls for police service. He has every right to expect a courteous response. Put yourself in that position and think about what it is like. Policemen do tend to become gruff. Courtesy has to be learned. But once you get used to it, it comes automatically.

Part of the problem is the way the men deal with one another, which is usually friendly and informal. But policemen do not deal only with one another. They deal with the public. Internally, there can be a certain amount of fun, a lot of camaraderie. We can call each other names because that is part of the fun and it helps to keep the ship afloat; but the public is not in a mood for fun and games when it becomes necessary to call a police department.

Thus, officers must be professional, businesslike, and courteous. It sounds simple, but it involves a very basic truth about human nature. People respond in kind. If one party is courteous, the other is more likely to be. That is what we have strived to instill in our men.

SHARING THE GLORY

The chief executive cannot worry about who gets the glory. That goes for any kind of glory. Glory has to be shared, and it can be, easily; its supply is inexhaustible. When the leader knows that, he is on his way to gaining the support and respect of his subordinates.

No one glorifies himself by putting down his subordinates. There was one of my bosses who could not see this. One day he said, "Will you drive me out to such-and-such a place? We are going to present a 25-year pin to Susie So-and-so, the secretary at such-and-such division." The division was having a cake-cutting ceremony, and the people out there asked the deputy chief to get in the picture with Susie. Inspector Davis, too. (Usually, it was, "Inspector Davis, you stand over there." You know the drill.) We did what we were told and they took our picture. It appeared in the monthly magazine.

After the picture was taken, my boss told me, "Inspector, I'll stay out of your pictures if you stay out of mine." Suddenly, it was clear. The great glory of having your picture taken at Susie so-and-so's 25th anniversary on the department and having your picture in the department magazine was some kind of a thrill to this dumb jerk. After that, when picture-taking time would come, a smart guy would say, "I'm going to find the head," then he'd look back around the corner, and when all the photographers were gone, he'd come back and say, "Chief, are you ready to go back to headquarters?"

There were also the pictures in the local newspapers as I was on my way up. There would be a huge seizure of narcotics, and some high-ranking detective chief or the sheriff would have his foot on this ton of marijuana or trunk full of heroin. The photographers would take a picture of this guy for the papers. Now, hard-working narcotics officers risked their lives and worked damn hard on that arrest. But who got in the papers? The sheriff, or some chief. He took all the credit. Yet most people are sophisticated enough to look at that photograph of the chief getting that kind of credit and realize that he could not be out doing all those things and still give all those speeches he gives. So they know that he is a phony.

The real glory can mean a hell of a lot to that guy on the narcotics squad, because he earned it. It can mean a lot to his immediate family, and he can make a lot of copies to send to relatives. There is an unlimited amount of glory and approbation available in this world, so a leader, right down to the rank of first-line supervisor, should never hesitate to acknowledge that someone has accomplished something good.

There are a lot of people who worry about their subordinates' getting any credit or any kind of attention. They somehow feel that there is a limited supply of glory. But let me tell you, glory—or credit, or approbation, or whatever you want to call it—is in infinite supply in this world. It is something we will never run out of. We can afford as much glory as we want for anybody.

A good mother and a good father give credit to their children. A boss who isn't willing to give credit to his subordinates, to build them up and be proud of them, is not really a good boss. The organization will never have any pride in that atmosphere. Most managers do not hesitate in taking a disciplinary action or entering a negative comment on a man's evaluation report. Yet they are often very slow about reducing to writing something that was really good. Why is that? Many of us are that way with our wives and our kids. We are that way with our neighbors and even our pets. We would be much better people and this would be a happier world if we were willing to give praise and not worry about doing it. The man who gives praise does not subtract praise from himself. That seems pretty obvious. But we just seem to hoard praise as it there were not going to be any of it left.

I have found that I do not give enough praise. Frequently, I will make out an evaluation on one of my assistant chiefs and he will say, "Boss, this is really great. I am going to work like the dickens to try and earn it." It becomes clear to me that I have rated him every six months and haven't told him during that time why I think so highly of him.

This habit of not praising is easy to fall into, but it is also easy to correct. All we have to do is begin giving more praise. After all, people like to know that their efforts are appreciated, and they like to know that others think they are something special. After the praise is dispensed, and once the guy receiving it begins to believe that it was really meant for him, watch the performance level. If it doesn't increase and crime doesn't decrease, I will eat the table of contents of this book.

PERSONAL HEALTH

For good reasons, it is vital that a leader feel fit and healthy. A person who doesn't feel fit cannot effectively lead an organization. I can recall working for people who are in pain, who were in bad health, or who were so concerned about themselves that they had to pace themselves. A police organization cannot tolerate that. It can have nothing less than good health throughout all ranks, but especially among its leaders.

We have pension systems for people who are not physically well. In Los Angeles, everyone hired for a policeman's job is in pretty good shape. But keeping in good shape for 20, 25, or 30 years is really a responsibility of the individual. Policemen, in general, tend to become lardbottoms after a while, usually because they sit on their duffs in a patrol car or behind a desk. And people in the community are constantly trying to fatten them up, always with good intentions.

Two things in particular work against sound health; one is physical inaction, and the other is an overabundance of food and drink. Inaction on the job can cause someone to become unhealthy who might function normally in one of those occupations with exercise, such as a service-station attendant or mailman, or even a housewife. A person in a sedentary occupation must get out several times a week in some kind of exercise to remain fit and healthy. If he is lucky, he can play golf five days a week; if he can't play golf, then he has to follow some other kind of daily exercise program.

I have tried to run at least one mile every working day for the last 25 years, and it has been my salvation. I would never have made it as chief during the last seven years if I did not put that daily run of one mile first on my agenda. When I get up in the morning, I put on my running trunks and running shoes and go out there with a stopwatch and run a mile. One of my close friends, a retired Marine officer, swims about a mile a day in the ocean. This guy is in his middle sixties and he is in excellent shape from a cardiovascular standpoint. He was on the Olympic water polo team back in 1932, and he has remained in good condition throughout his life.

People who rise to positions of authority can really hold their organization back because of their lethargy. If they don't feel good, they will pass that attitude on to their people. If they do feel good, if they have worked out, first thing in the morning particularly, they pass on a totally different attitude. The healthy leader feels he can whip a whole cage of tigers. It is critical to a uniformed policeman who is sitting there picking up all that weight in that radio car, or a manager, to get that old cardiovascular system going every day.

My whole department is now required to be in shape, and each man takes a periodic physical fitness test. The test is administered at every division, and if a man can't do a certain number of pushups and situps, or achieve a certain pulse rate after performing a step test, then he flunks and that fact goes on his personal evaluation report.

There is no on-duty time to get in shape. That is the man's own responsibility. It is a liability for the city if you have everybody conditioning themselves on city time. And pension liabilities can go up. When we put this program together, we had a few casualties. One was a young guy in his mid-thirties, a weight lifter with great big muscles to boot, who looked as though he was in good shape, but when he started running, he couldn't perform. He had never conditioned his cardiovascular system, even though he had those big muscles. But the ones who remain, and there are many survivors, are in a lot better shape and feel a lot better. My department is more vigorous and a better organization because of it. Particularly, the brass are in better shape.

We also put all my higher-ranking men on the running treadmill once a year. We get them on there and hook up the heartbeat device and the blood-pressure device and the respiration device. We turn the machine on and they can see what it would take to kill them. And when they are getting out of shape, either I have to personally give them hell or their particular boss does. Since the program was initiated, we haven't had one casualty among the top brass. We have been able to get them all to change their way of living, whatever way they have to change it.

We accomplished that at very little investment for my city, with the potential savings pegged at much more, both in more years of service and fewer disability pensions. Now when we start out on some new program, we look around and find that more of my general staff have the energy and enthusiasm to keep up with me. That is very satisfying.

KNOWLEDGE OF THE PERSONAL REWARDS

There are some disadvantages to serving in the highest position within a police agency. In all probability, the financial rewards, including the pension and all the other economic rewards, are not as great as the sacrifice. When the length of working hours and the workload itself are considered, there is probably very little difference between the top executive and the one perhaps one or two steps below that position, at least from a monetary standpoint. The solitude of the job and the requirement that the effective leader devote almost 100 percent of his time to it usually preclude his making any extra money. Generally, most investments—whether in real estate, stock, or any other type of venture—require more management time and effort than he is able to give.

So no one should ever seek the job of chief executive solely for the reason of personal monetary reward. A great many police chiefs have come and gone in my seven years in the top spot and in my ten years as an officer of the International Association of Chiefs of Police. I have yet to see one who has done as well financially as most of his subordinates who have the time to look after their own interests. What that means, then, is that during the selection process for a chief executive, this willingness to sacrifice material and financial rewards must be sought as a qualification of the candidate. It also means that the candidate, certainly the dedicated one, must know going in what he will be required to neglect his investments for the good of the organization. If he does not, he will disappoint himself or the organization when he achieves the top spot.

Another reason that those making the selection for the top spot need to recognize this situation is that the new chief executive should have sufficient salary to be able to sacrifice his other interests, and to preclude him from becoming involved in shady deals or "get-rich-quick" schemes because he is not making enough money.

SUMMARY

To summarize the more personal aspects of leadership, health must be maintained and financial sacrifice must be recognized. It takes guts to tell someone in a powerful position that he is wrong and that you are going to do something to correct him. It takes a special insight, and experience, to be able to recognize the motives and feelings of others and deal sensitively with these human emotions.

I think I know where leaders ought to come from— within an organization—and from outside an organization, when that is necessary. Also, after more than 35 years in a profession absolutely dependent upon good leadership, I have an idea what it takes to develop a good leader. A very special combination of factors go into making a leader in my profession. In essence, that is what this chapter has been all about.

10

Executive Peace

TECHNIQUES FOR ACHIEVING PEACE OF MIND

A number of people over the years have told me, "God, I am glad I don't have your job. You have such great responsibilities. A city of three million people and more than ten thousand employees. I read in the paper about all these people criticizing you and you having to fight one battle after another. You must be ready to give up." People say that all the time but it simply isn't true.

Maintaining Standards

Frankly, mine isn't really a difficult job. I am constantly at peace with myself because I do all the things I am supposed to do, when I am supposed to do them. I never let anything hang over and interfere with some other problem. I have peace of mind because I always try to do the right thing even if it is the more difficult thing to do.

Sometimes a leader is tempted to intercede, for example, in an arrest situation involving a very important person. My simple solution to that dilemma is—Never! If the mayor or the governor is arrested in my city, we will process him and prosecute him just as we would anyone else.

We arrested a deputy mayor in our city in 1975—a very unfortunate situation, because there is no joy in seeing a man destroy himself, especially if he is a reasonably good administrator. He was successfully prosecuted in municipal court for his crime. That doesn't always happen everywhere. My department has also arrested judges without serious consequences. You simply do not worry about having any skeletons in the police department closet, because such things are not covered up. Each tough decision that comes along is dealt with reasonably, ethically, and properly.

Occasionally there might be a certain temptation to compromise, to take the easy path, or to be nice and sweet and cooperate with a United States House or Senate investigating committee. When that happens, you have to remind them that under the Tenth Amendment to the Constitution, they have no damn business sticking their noses in the department. I have told them that if they really want to investigate something, they might consider sticking their noses in their own tents. As an executive, I can live with that kind of problem, because the Constitution helps to bring me peace by providing for a separation of powers. If an executive meets his problems every day—even if the problem is the United States Congress—and disposes of them every day, on the basis of principle, and tries to be as forgiving and loving as he can in addition to being tough when he has to make tough decisions, he will have peace of mind.

I am generally perceived as having a pretty good memory. I can remember infinitely tiny details of things, much like a computer. But I have a terrible problem remembering who my enemies are. I will see some guy and remember having been really mad at him a few years ago. Yet I cannot remember what it was about. The concept of executive peace is founded upon principles rather than personalities, and that is very important.

Today's Business Today

Another basis for this peace is that the executive should not carry the burdens of yesterday with him today, because each new day is going to produce more burdens. Every day's burdens must, therefore, be handled that same day. I do not believe in participating in the in-basket game. My desk has no drawers; it is just a plain, flat table. That is by design. When there is something sent out to be done, it will eventually come to me in a week or so. When it comes back, I examine it; if it is good, it goes forward; if it is poor, I give it back to the subordinate with instructions on how he is to do it, and he gets a new deadline. But nothing stays with me overnight. I don't have to worry about a project: Either it is done and goes forward, or it is not done and somebody else needs to worry about it. But me, I don't worry.

As a result, there are no problems that are left for tomorrow. There are no projects to carry home in a briefcase to read. They are read at my desk, and they are either ready or they are not ready. The only things carried home in my briefcase are letters from citizens. There is considerable value in the insights that are received from the public, and I sometimes get behind in my correspondence and neglect to get those letters read every day. However, the concept of doing every day's work today and never having yesterday's problems on your mind is extremely important to an executive's peace of mind.

The principle of handling your work on a daily basis will be taken up in more detail in Chapter Fourteen, but let me describe what happens to people who do not resolve problems on a daily basis. They weasel around and avoid making decisions. As each new problem arises, they find that they are preoccupied and worried about another problem that has been sitting for so long that it is now stinking. Then they put the problems of today on top of those older problems, and they end up with a huge reserve of problems in the back of their minds that really begins to worry them, eventually becoming intolerable.

Organizing Your Time

A police chief executive, just like any other executive, should be the master of his own day with respect to organizing the time spent at any given task or responsibility. Mornings are the most creative time of the day for me, and they are reserved for personal work. My day is organized in the following fashion: My first few moments in the office, providing that I do not have to return any important phone calls that have been received that morning, are spent in dictation, which I keep up on a daily basis.

Next, my executive officer comes in with the mail that has been directed to the office since the last time he was in to see me. This correspondence is from both within and outside the department. My executive officer recommends certain routing for important mail. Some of it will be routed to other offices, and some of it will be handled by me. Some pieces of the mail have been directed to an appropriate place before this review process; this would be routine mail, or information dealing with crime statistics, for example. If we received a letter requesting certain information on training, say, that letter would not be called to my attention; it would automatically be forwarded to the appropriate office. If it had to do with a major policy question or some other request of major significance, it would be brought to my attention.

If I agree with the routing, the instructions given to the person responsible for drafting a reply, the deadline, and other considerations, the letter is forwarded to that unit in the department. When the letter returns to my office at a later date, it will be examined closely for its responsiveness and content. If it is not responsive, it goes back to the writer.

After I work with the executive officer, there is usually some time available for seeing top members of my staff, my assistant chiefs or members of my personal staff who are responsible for material transmitted to the board of police commissioners. I try to avoid filling the middle part of my day, the lunch hour, with speeches. Luncheon speeches steal a very prime part of the day. They require about 30 minutes of transportation time, 90 minutes of luncheon and speaking time, and another 30 minutes of transportation time coming back. There are more important work demands that should take priority over this 2½ hours, most of it spent with a group of people who generally just want to be entertained. There are exceptions; I do give some luncheon speeches, but I try to avoid them and use the luncheon time to have a sandwich at my desk with someone, or some group, from the community who thinks it has a specific problem. Whether it is an Arab group, a Jewish group, or a Korean group, or perhaps media people, I try to meet at that time with them, scheduling these informal little lunches either in a separate dining room or at my desk. It offers a great opportunity to gain new insights and new input from important segments of the community.

In the afternoon, there is generally a prescheduled meeting with one of my top executives, since each of them has his own scheduled time to see me each week. I spend some afternoons in vertical staff meetings, meeting with a particular organizational segment of the department. Another afternoon might be spent listening to people in the policeman rank. The important part of these meetings, as mentioned previously, is listening.

When the executive's time is used in this manner, planned out carefully, dealing immediately with specific tasks rather than allowing a daily intrusion of multiple problems, more can be accomplished. The purpose of organizing the executive's day in the manner discussed here, organizing by time allocation, is that the leader becomes the master of the ship. The other alternative would require his being at the beck and call of others: When a letter was delivered, someone would bring it to him and he would act on it. Then a telephone call would come in and he would act on that. Perhaps a subordinate might come in with a minor problem and he would act on that. The executive would not be able to plan his day; events and the affairs of others would do it for him. Everyone else is able to plan his own day, so why should others be allowed to plan the executive's day? Nobody plans my day but me.

There were a couple of years when others were able to dominate my time and work, and it damn near killed me. I told my secretary and I told my wife, "To hell with that! I'm going to run my own damn life, and those people who want to come in and take all my time starting at nine o'clock in the morning, I'm going to see how long they want to talk when they get an appointment at five-thirty at night." I found myself in the office at eight at night, doing the paperwork that should have been completed at ten in the morning, and getting home at nine or ten in the evening. I decided to just turn the whole thing around, and now I am in charge of my time.

I don't run the police department; I just see that the police department is run well. Father Lees, the president of Chaminade College in Hawaii, once said, "I don't run the university or the college. I just see that it's run properly." And that is what a good chief of police does. He doesn't have to make every little decision every five minutes. All he has to do is see that the department is being run properly by all the managers who are receiving good money to fulfill their responsibilities. You were always able to find Chief Parker late at night in his office, but you couldn't find any of the deputy chiefs in theirs. If you had had a wire strung along outside their offices, they would all have fallen on their faces exactly at five o'clock. Now, if they want to see me and they don't have a scheduled time, they have to see me at five and five-thirty in the afternoon. It's amazing how brief they are at five-thirty—a lot briefer than they are when they can get in and entertain me at nine in the morning.

I have simply decided that I'm going to have peace and tranquility, and nobody's going to steal my time. There are only a few exceptions; my wife, for instance, when she calls is immediately put through to me. I can now tell her, "Yes, ma'am, I will make it home on time." She has number one priority. The mayor, and president of the police commission, or any great emergency I should know about are also exceptions. But really, there are not very many great emergencies. In fact, most emergencies are created by the media, which means they are generally artificial, contrived, or pseudo events. Random access to the chief executive, that so-called open-door policy, where everyone can walk in whenever they want to, prevents the effective leader from getting his work done. It is a nice, attractive concept, but it is not practical in a large police department.

I do have a planned open-door policy. It is limited, however, to meetings in the afternoon, when people can confide in me and tell me how screwed up things are in the police department. Yet I control it, it does not control me. I gain insight into everyday problems and share things with people, but I am the master of my time.[1]

Generally, this applies also to any policeman in my department who says he simply must see the chief. If my secretary finds five or ten minutes that day, I will try to see or

[1]The reader might consider the fundamental truth of Parkinson's Law, which explains that work tends to expand to fill the time available; thus, the amount of work depends upon the availability of time.

talk to that officer. The men within the department respect my situation, and they very seldom abuse it.

Occasionally people of lower rank get in that way, but generally I can see them in the vertical staff meetings. That way I get a lot more bang for the buck. The general open-door policy where everyone comes and goes, in an organization of large size, is one of the most foolish myths ever perpetrated on an executive. If he really has an open door and if people really can dominate his time, then he isn't going to be the chief executive, he is going to be the chief chaplain of the organization.

What it gets down to is that you must set blocks of time to do certain important and specific things, and you must stick to that schedule. Then, if anyone just has to see you and if you are scheduled to get through about five-thirty or six o'clock, they can see you at five-thirty or six. The first thing they say will be, "You know, Boss, this will only take about a minute," and sure enough, it does only take a minute. That same person would take about 30 minutes with the same problem at nine o'clock in the morning. But now, because his wife is going to get angry with him if he is late for dinner, it is only going to take a minute.

Before I had this change in schedule, my wife had to put my dinner in the oven. No more! I would get home at nine or ten for a warmed-over meal that had been prepared and ready for a decent serving at six or seven. My wife was unhappy with me, and I really felt bad. But no more. We have been utilizing this method now for six of my eight years as chief.

Time is critically important to an executive, and he must control it. He must also remember that he is not running the outfit; he is responsible for seeing that it is run properly. He cannot place himself in the position of being required to make every decision, large or small. If he falls into that trap, he is not really filling the role of chief executive. He is being the subordinate to some other person who has, by virtue of controlling his time, become the real chief executive.

Utilizing Subordinates

Another executive technique that has been very helpful to me is moving a subordinate into my job whenever I am required to be away from the office. Thus, when I return, there are no little problems waiting for me. I do expect a short report from the acting chief executive, by way of a tape recording that fully describes in 30 or 40 minutes all the highlights and a blow-by-blow account of the important occurrences during my absence. It is my own view that an acting chief executive should be able to review and approve those matters that should go to the mayor, or to the city council, or to the commission; he should be willing and able to take disciplinary action; in effect, the acting chief executive should handle it all.

The previous chief of police in my department would appoint an acting chief of police who was contacted in the event of an emergency. However, while the chief was out of town, all his work was backing up and being neglected. When he returned, he would be totally overwhelmed. For that reason, I put in the move-up system. The assistant chief physically moves into my office and does my job. Then a deputy chief moves into *his* office, a commander moves into the deputy chief's office, and so on, right on down to where a sergeant moves up into a lieutenant's job. Policemen don't move into the sergeant's job, but everyone's work is going on every day regardless of whether he is there. The job goes on. It is not just suspended until some little tin god gets back, because none of us are gods and we shouldn't act as though we are. By using the move-up system, an agency or organization is able to move forward all the time at the same steady pace instead of waiting until the top man gets back.

Not only does the organization receive the advantage of continuous progress, but there is the added benefit of ongoing executive development. Young men who want to get ahead in the organization are given an opportunity to experience the task ahead of them. A captain is able to go out and do a commander's job for a month while the commander is on vacation. A sergeant does the lieutenant's job for a month while the lieutenant attends a special training program. And the acting chief can make the same decisions the chief would make if he were there. Anyone who says he is going to have something for the chief when he comes back is a very inadequate leader and shouldn't go much farther ahead. *He should be evaluated as poor.*

When a ballplayer is at bat and that pitch comes across, he had better make a decision as to whether to wait and hope it is called a ball or swing at it and try his best to hit it. Every batter in my department, even the pinch hitter, is up at bat all the time, and he is expected to be a real hitter. He is out there to hit just like the regular hitter even when the regular hitter isn't there. The very real danger in an organization is that there is no time to wait for things to get done until after the boss gets back. Organizations that wait for the boss are going to keep on waiting, because bosses acquire all kinds of problems along the way. Soon they become very depressed, and they may even lose their jobs because they become overwhelmed. If too many problems queue up, no man is going to be able to handle them.

The Control System

Let me describe what some executives have done on their way up through the organization. A man was given by his boss a very difficult assignment that he did not really believe in. The boss said, "I want something written, an order or some bulletin, that indicates how this thing works." The subordinate thought, "Gee, I don't know how to do that. I don't even know how to start it." The project went into the in-basket, and every day the subordinate got down to that point in the basket and spotted the thing. Pretty soon it began to bother him. After a while he got so embarrassed about it that he took it out and put it in a "Hold" file in his top desk drawer—a special place where he kept current matters. He looked through this drawer every day too, and soon he was even more embarrassed, because the thing was still there. So he put it in the bottom drawer, down where he kept the Kleenex, his shoeshine stuff, and his executive tool kit. One day, while he was shining his shoes, he saw this piece of paper. By now it was moldy, and he said, "My goodness, this monster has been here for six months. The old man must have forgotten about it." He promptly tore it up, threw it in the wastebasket, and hoped that the boss really had forgotten it and had not made a record of it. He sat on pins and needles for a year, until he was finally and absolutely sure it had been forgotten.

This tale brings two things to mind. First, the executive who assigned the work should have had a control system. When I assign something to a guy, I give him a "DWI"—not a due date, a "due *within* date," meaning do it faster if you can. Periodically, when projects are not in on time, my executive officer presents me with a deficiency list. I get on the phone or write a nasty little note saying, "Deputy Chief So-and-so, why isn't this project here? It was due today. Where is it? I did not say to have it in here today; I said that it was due *by* this date. You just flunked when you failed to get that to me today." Control systems are a must in organizations.

Second, the personal staff of the executive must be able to deal with the subordinates in the other staff offices and interpret to them what the executive wants. People who claim to be trying to figure out what the executive really wants are usually just asking for help with their project. They either do not know what they are doing or they are trying to get someone else to do some of their work. In my case, I usually want exactly what I say I want. When I assign a task, I do not want people to give me only what I already know about the matter. I want them to give me a solution to a problem, using their best judgment, imagination, and detailed insight. If I had wanted to solve the problem myself, it would not have been sent out to someone else.

People are often too concerned about pleasing the boss. The boss is generally pleased when he learns that someone has exercised a little judgment and research time to properly develop a problem and detail some very rational alternatives that might be utilized in resolving it.

Mastering the Telephone

Some executives can totally isolate themselves, control access to themselves by people who try to physically get in to take their time. Such bosses have got pretty well pegged all the windbags who come in just to rap, guys who can really screw up the whole day. Some executives have gone so far as to remove all the chairs from their offices to prevent people from sitting down and getting comfortable. But these same executives will accept a phone call from practically anyone and everyone, particularly if it is long distance.

If you answered all the long-distance telephone calls that come into your office, you would never get any work done. Someone will buzz you on the intercom and say that So-and-so, a personal friend, is calling from, say, Boston, Massachusetts. Well, there is no need to talk to him just because it is a long-distance phone call. If you know the guy in Boston, and it is important to the police department, fine, talk to him. But before you do, have someone screen the call, because nearly everyone who calls will say that he has to talk to the chief. More often than not, a sergeant can do them more good than the chief of police.

Or a call may come in from someone who wants to become a police officer, asking what the next filing date is, or what forms a candidate is required to complete. The chief doesn't know the answers, but he has people who do know. The staff should get those routine telephone calls and refer them to the proper person. The chief doesn't know everything, so people who call him directly to resolve something within the department are probably making a poor choice.

The good executive's staff should be capable of referring a caller to an expert in whatever specific area the call is about.

You can always return the phone calls that are vital. Calls from the governor or his immediate subordinates, the police commissioners, the mayor, and your wife are the really important ones.

Every person has his own definition of peace. To sky-divers, for instance, it may be those few moments when they are alone in the sky, plummeting toward the earth, in one of the most dangerous sports known—but that is their peace. To a police chief—to me, anyway—it is stopping for a moment and seeing that things are working right, and then jumping right back into the action.

Some of the matters I have discussed here are naturally part of being a leader, but more specifically, they reflect my way of coming to terms with "the system." They are tricks of my trade that have brought me through some of the tough spots in my tenure as police chief of one of the most dynamic organizations I know of—the Los Angeles Police Department.

SELF-DIRECTION

When you get into the top spot, nobody can really tell you what to do. You are the player/coach. No one else is going to send in the signals. The effective leader has to be self-directed and self-motivated. This motivation comes from being constantly aware of every threat to the community and to the organization.

A chief of police has to be immediately on top of the prime happenings around his city. That doesn't mean he has to know about every burglary, but he had better know the burglary trends on at least a weekly basis. He has to have readings on what the vice situation is, not just from the vice squad, but from somebody who checks up on the vice squad— and even from someone who checks up on *them,* like an inspection and control unit. He has to have enough input from down below, by listening to policemen and people of various ranks, so that he knows what is going on. He has to constantly take the necessary steps to redirect the efforts and energies of the organization.

When the chief doesn't have this sense of what is happening, he can fail to change direction, and then serious long-term drifts occur. If these continue, they can eventually result in the nearly total destruction of morale and esprit de corps of an organization. Organizations may go on for a long time this way, disregarding all the rocks, shoals, and sandbars, and eventually cracking up. Getting an organization like that moving again is extremely difficult for anyone.

The leader cannot afford confusion. Anyone who is confused by what is happening cannot and should not be in that kind of a position. Believe me, one thing that you can count on in a large city is being surprised every day of your life. There are never two days alike. Just when you say nothing more can happen, it will. If you respond to every crisis adequately, the ship will be guided properly to the right waters. If a leader does not have his own internal guidance system, he will not be able to make that response.

LEVERAGE

Leverage is the amount of force utilized at a fulcrum to move a greater weight. An effective administrator should have a policy that permits him to use human leverage in every way he can. Never do anything the hard way. Always attempt, where possible, to condition things so that there are several people helping you to move that weight.

An excellent example is the use of public involvement in crime prevention, public involvement in crime deterrence, and public involvement in criminal apprehension. If you have the public looking for bad guys and providing information, you as the executive can be more effective. The police cannot do the job by themselves.

Another example is involvement of the men through a police association, which can accomplish much to better the department. If a union has the same goals as the organization in some area, then it can really help.

Wherever possible, you should do things with the greatest amount of support possible. You will soon get very tired if you try to do it all yourself. Policemen out in the street, all over the world, are too frequently trying to do the job by themselves instead of making use of a potentially tremendous amount of public cooperation. As a result, not only is their job more difficult, but they feel along.

As a young man, working for my city planting and removing trees, I learned this valuable lesson in the most elementary way. I could work all day by myself, concocting some elaborate scheme to unearth a big tree and get it out of the ground. Or I could construct a rather simple lifting device that could be used with eight or ten people. That way, the tree was out and on the truck in a matter of minutes.

That's leverage. In a more specific sense, it was the beginning of my quest for peace of mind. I got more satisfaction in knowing that I had kept my partners working than in satisfying some egotistical urge to prove that I could do the job alone without any help. That is how I view executive peace now after all these years. I have had my share of it.

III
POLICE MANAGEMENT

11

Organizing
for Police Management

TYPES OF ORGANIZATIONS

At least until recently, the organization has generally been
depicted in most textbooks, and in many of the schools of
administration, as a flat scale comprising line and staff structures. There is one level of top brass, one level of managers,
and one level of supervisors. The workers of the organization
are always at the bottom and the bosses at the top.

That might appeal to some, but an organization can also
be thought of the other way around, with the working
people—the ones who do the job, the important ones—at
the top. Those who make it possible for them to go in the

right direction and to function in the organizational mode, through training, selection, and expression of policies—that is, the supervisors—are the appendages in this upside-down type of structure, so they go below.

Today, I think of a police organization in a third way—as being like a sphere, a big ball. The people in contact with the real world—the investigators and the policemen, the work force—are along the exterior edge of that ball. The staff support elements are a little bit further toward the center and the brass and the chief executive are nearest the center (see chart on page 128). In this type of structure, the executives are not as far from the workers as they are in the scalar chart. The individuals within the organization are like molecules that compose this sphere, and they go around and around, touching other molecules at one point or another. A good organization is a sphere in which every element on the inside, whether it is the chief or another member of the brass or an instructor at the academy, is sufficiently in touch with all the other parts. This kind of movement permits every part of the entire sphere to be in contact with both the outside world and the core of the sphere.

That seems to me to be a real, living organization. In a sense, that is why I have such a dislike and distrust for the traditional chain of command. To a certain extent it may be an overreaction. I do try to recognize the importance of the chain of command, but no effective leader should become so impressed with himself and so hung up on form and detail that people are forced to go around him.

There have always been different types of informal communication; whatever the organizational mode, there will be rumors and scuttlebutt and informal meetings. If the working people think they are being excluded from knowing what the brass is thinking and doing, they will have their own meetings and talk about it. With any luck, some of the brass might be there, and a better kind of external and informal communication will take place. The organizational structure should enhance this type of communication, and even formalize it, so that it occurs in the natural course of duties.

We should have much greater intercommunication than is generally perceived to occur in organizations. To do that, we must get the traditional type of thinking on organization out of our heads. We should begin to think of the organization as a facilitator of communication rather than a formal monolith.

Now, many of the standard, reliable principles of organization, such as span of control, still have some value. Even the chain of command can have some value; there will always be a need for all the positions between working people and the top brass, but they cannot be allowed to become calcified. The middle brass produce nothing in and of themselves, and one of the most difficult things we have to do is get the people in between the workers and the top brass to realize that they are servants of the people—servants of the working people and servants of the leadership.

Unfortunately, some people, when they get promoted within an organization, hit a place where the altitude is so high for them that it blows them all out of shape. The air is too rarefied for them. They become so inflated with their own importance and their attitudes that little gets done. This is the plateau concept, what Dr. Lawrence Peter called the "Peter Principle."[1] It is the point at which a person reaches his "level of incompetence."

When you have a chain of command that requires that everything go up and down through it, it will soon become unable to function. People who perceive their role as merely a part of the chain of command, rather than as that of a facilitator, are going to become deterrents to organizational effectiveness. They may be happy with their role, and they may feel that they have found their place in the sun, but the organization will be dying for lack of sunlight.

In the upside-down organization, the brass expends its efforts toward making the working level more effective, instead of vice versa. Once that is perceived, and the working-

[1] L.J. Peter and R. Hull, *The Peter Principle* (New York: Bantam Books, 1969).

OFFICE OF OPERATIONS MANAGEMENT TEAM

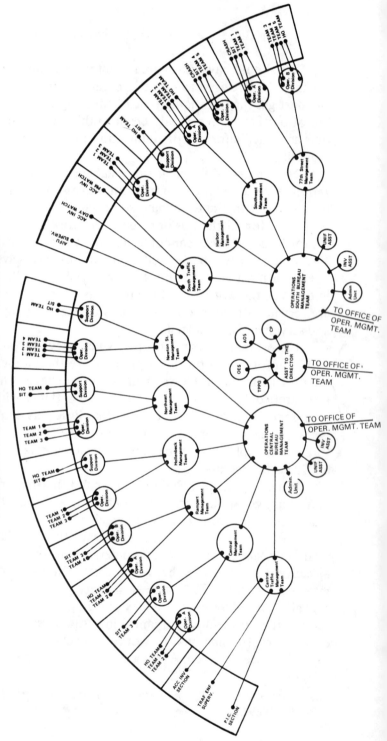

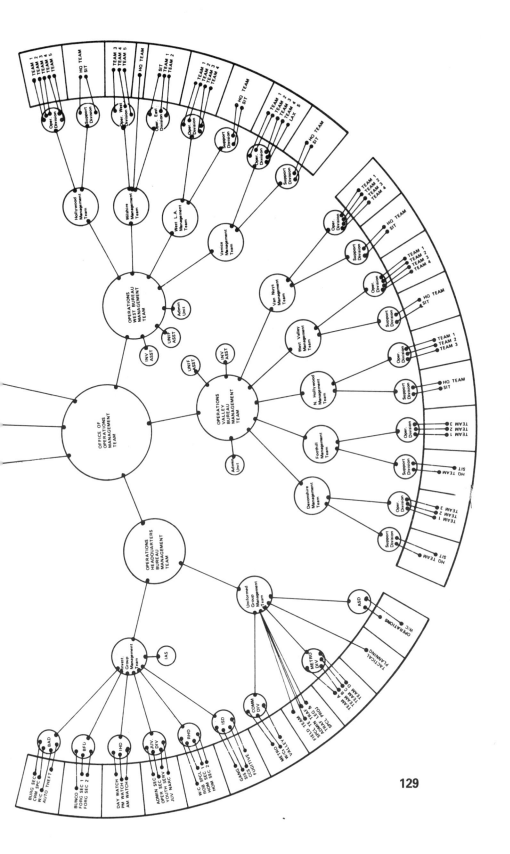

129

level people get the idea that someone is there to help, both the brass and the workers will accomplish what they set out to do.

PROPERLY PACED CHANGE

Because the world is always changing, change is vital to the proper operation of any organization. But that does not mean that we have to change our principles; we may have to change techniques, but not principles. We might even have to change the rules, because very little on earth remains static, except perhaps our value system relating to our Creator.

If you are driving a car down a straight road, pointed in a certain direction, you can go off course if you fail to make corrections in the alignment of the wheels, because there are all kinds of little bumps and wind currents that can throw the car off. While you drive, you are constantly sorting information. You are correcting the steering wheel of the car and depressing or releasing the accelerator to make changes. That is the only way of safely operating a vehicle. In involves a constant set of corrections.

An organization must also be constantly making changes. And virtually all major changes, and even minor ones, even if they are welcomed, can be traumatic. We are creatures of habit, and our feeling of security is based on doing things the same way we did them before. The routine way of doing things is a security blanket to all creatures. Whenever you force a change on a human or any other creature, you have problems.

When an administrator attempts to effect change in an organization, he is guiding his ship to unknown waters where there may be a great many rocks. In deep water one must be cautious of huge swells and heavy waves, because there is a great chance that the boat may be swamped. So the method of change has to be smooth.

An organization can't remain the same in every detail and survive. Down through history, all organisms change to adapt themselves to their environment, and organizations have to change or they go out of business. Unfortunately, public organizations aren't usually forced to change, because of the absence of free-market pressures, so they tend to become calcified and protective of their own survival.

When I was a little boy, the grocery store my family shopped at was very different from the kind you see today. Like most people back then, we usually shopped once a week. When we came in, the grocer would put a cardboard box on the counter and fill it, item by item, with the things my mother asked for—two boxes of oatmeal, three cans of soup, and so on—fetching each item by hand or with a grabber on a long stick. When the box was filled, my dad would pay him about five dollars—a lot of money then—and the grocer would carry the box out to the car.

Today, we shop in supermarkets, where we walk in and serve ourselves. The clerks put the items on the shelves and the customer does all the rest of the work. With today's labor costs, if we had to send someone all over the store to get what we ordered, we wouldn't be able to afford the price of food. Personal service has given way to efficiency and cost-effectiveness.

Unlike the grocery business, many police departments are still being run exactly the same way they were run 50 years ago—in the same buildings, in many cases. They still have a night watch, a day watch, and a morning watch. They also have a patrol bureau, a traffic bureau, and a detective bureau. They do everything about the same way; even their policies haven't changed very much. If the grocery business had continued to merchandise groceries the way it did 50 years ago, it would be broke—or its customers would. However, government organizations can be absolutely incompetent and still remain in business. It is really too bad that there isn't some way of forcing change on them, instead of having them exist into perpetuity in all their glorious incompetence.

Change is necessary; *how much* change depends on how regularly change occurs. Once an organization has been brought to a modern state, it won't need many changes. It will be much like moving the wheel of a car imperceptibly as you drive down the freeway; you hardly notice the changes in the steering wheel. In addition, change must be achieved with as much knowledge and understanding of the people at the bottom and up through the middle as possible. Even then, it will still be painful to someone. Also, change should be accomplished as slowly as is practicable. A brilliant observer of management, a man named Fritz Roethlisberger, suggested that the best way of achieving change is to think about it like the mortar between bricks. You could change all the mortar between the bricks in an old building if you did it gradually, by taking the mortar out of each place in turn and immediately filling the void with new mortar. You would eventually change all the mortar in that whole building without ever structurally weakening the building at all. But, he said, if you took all the mortar out at once, the building would collapse.[2]

That is a pretty good analogy on how to bring about change. Don't remove all the mortar from between the bricks at one time. Whether it is simply changing the hours of work or making an organizational change, like the difference between team policing and watch policing, introduce the change slowly and deliberately.

All the changes my department has gone through in the last seven years have been extremely slow—agonizingly slow to many members of the department. But we had to do it that way. We tried to do it gradually and we tried to get as many of the people as possible involved in the task. In February 1975, my department implemented full team policing. We had taken about five years to make the total transition, but it was continuous. We started warming up with the Basic-Car

[2]F. Roethlisberger and W.J. Dickson, *Management and the Worker* (Cambridge, Mass.: Harvard University Press, 1939).

Plan in January 1970. All men participated. We took our police officers to the academy, where they could all meet together and discuss how they were going to bring about the change. Some teams even went to Lake Arrowhead, in the mountains, to hold team conferences. There was tremendous involvement.

In spite of all that, there were still some who said, "They screwed up the whole department." Some felt they had to leave; they just couldn't stand it any more. It is tough for some people to stay in a place if everything around them is changing—the kinds of calls they answer, whom they work for, what they do every day, and who works with them. When all these things change, it can become a very traumatic experience.

My point here is that you must change to survive and to properly serve, but true and effective change must involve participation and understanding of change, and it must be gradual and deliberate. Further, it is necessary to recognize the fact that there will be casualties even if everything is done correctly. A manager must simply fill up the ranks and go forward, already planning the next change.

My own experience has been that the toughest people to accommodate in change are in middle management. You can get the policemen to effect changes, and you can get your immediate assistants to go along. The greatest difficulty comes at the captain, lieutenant, and commander level, because these people are not doing the work at the line level and they are not making the decisions at the top. This is the dangerous area in the organization, and special attention should be given to trying to get middle managers as fully involved as possible in the process of change.

Another difficulty lies in getting older people to change. It is generally accepted that it is extremely hard, if not impossible, to change attitudes of people over 35. My experience is that there are great individual differences. Some people are very young at 75, and some are old fogies at 30. There are reactionary young people and very flexible older people. It isn't a question of age. For all of us, whether we are flexible or inflexible, change can be extremely traumatic.

But whether we like it or not, change is absolutely necessary. The only choice we face is whether we are going to change and survive or, like the dinosaur, refuse to change and die. Because government perpetuates incompetent, ineffective organizations, many totally out-of-date public organizations continue to survive and chew up vast sums of the taxpayers' dollars. They give a very small return on the investment, yet if they could adapt to change, they could maximize their return to the taxpayers.

The knowledge that change is inevitable, and the knowledge of how to bring it about organizationally, can produce peace of mind for every manager. Coping with rapid change and measuring its effect upon the organization are vital skills.

THE TERRITORIAL IMPERATIVE

When you examine living organisms in a natural setting, whether they are ants or lions or men, you see that each type has a special territory marked off for itself. A lion will have a certain area of turf where he is the master, and no other lion had better trespass on it. An ant family will dominate a certain amount of territory, and a foreign ant that invades that area will be repulsed. The same holds true for fish, birds, and man. Each one of us naturally identifies with an area. Certainly, one piece of turf most of us identify with is our homes. The home has become sacred to us, and others had better stay out unless they are invited in. This phenomenon was best described by the social anthropologist, Robert Ardrey, in his book, _The Territorial Imperative._[3]

The defending force of all animals and insects on their own turf is much stronger than that of an invading force

[3]Robert L. Ardrey, _Territorial Imperative: A Personal Inquiry into the Animal Origins of Property and Nations_ (New York: Atheneum, 1966).

trying to take it. The Viet Cong in South Vietnam, who identified with communism, were fiercely territorial in their feelings. They said, "This is our country! We're going to take it away from those people who believe in imperialism and we're going to convert it to a Marxist South Vietnam." All the might of America involved in that operation was unable to rid South Vietnam of those indigenous Viet Cong, let alone the invading armies from North Vietnam. However, if you took those same Viet Cong and put them in the Arizona desert and matched them up against the same number of American fighting men, the Americans would annihilate them. It's just a natural thing.

All through the history of the world, people have been subjugated and conquered, but they never really lost that feeling of turf. Sometime in the future, it may very well happen that the Lithuanians, the Czechoslovakians, and the Armenians will eventually get back their territory. All these people who have been subjugated by Russia are not totally assimilated at all. You can't go in and take over India without the Indians eventually, at some time in history saying, "India is for Indians! We're going to throw you British cats out." And they did. You see this idea at play in wars time after time, and anyone who forgets the rules of territorial imperative is doomed to some kind of trouble.

This theory can be related to police work. If we allow policemen to go anyplace they want to go within the confines of a small and specific area and tell them that they are responsible for every crime and traffic problem, they will be concerned. A burglary occurring in that area will have much the same impact as a personal crime against the officer.

The way we have used the concept of the territorial imperative is to deploy personnel into a Basic-Car District, where the policemen are confined to a certain district and held responsible for it. A short time after this was done, the Los Angeles Police Department extended the concept to all personnel by instituting team policing. Today, every one of my men out in the field, in general field work and general investigation, is a part of the "territorial imperative." If a pin goes up on a map indicating a burglary, it hurts each team member. They think, "*We* are being ripped off." It becomes a conflict between the team and the bad guys—us against them.

In addition to the policemen's being sensitive to the crime level, the people of that territory become *their people.* If the policeman is white and the people he serves are black, he may think at first, "I don't like black people very much," and the black people may think at first, "We don't like white cops very much." Yet he's their protector, and he knows that they are depending on him; and if they sit down and rap together about how to protect the area, pretty soon the whiteness and the blackness disappear, and it becomes *Us,* a feeling of unity. We, the police and the people of Watts, against the criminal army.

We put a team into Watts; it was called Team 29. (There was quite a bit of literature about the LAPD Team 28 in Venice, but the second team, Team 29, was in Watts.) Some time later, I was invited to lunch in a family's back yard in Watts. They had invited a lot of their neighbors in, and the community had invited Team 29. The people were telling me, these black people, "Team 29 is the greatest team in the department. Crime is down 50 percent in our neighborhood."

I said, "Oh, crime can't be down 50 percent. I can't believe that."

They said, "Wait, we'll get Tony." They got Tony.

Tony was a white motorcycle policeman with boots on. Normally, policemen with boots on aren't too concerned about burglaries and that sort of thing; they're concerned about traffic tickets. But Tony, as a part of the team, meeting with these people and having the people depend on him, was all enthused about reducing burglaries.

Well, it turned out I was right; crime wasn't really down 50 percent. It was only down about 30 percent, but at a time when crime was going up in almost every other city in America. At the end of one year in that district, with mostly white policemen and an almost totally black population, they had a

27 percent reduction in crime! When we tried to move any of those policemen out of that team, people would protest vehemently. "You can't take Tony, because Tony's a part of our protection!" We would say, "We have another guy just like Tony. We've got another guy just as good. Tony's making sergeant, and we have to take him away."

And then they said, "You're always doing that. You put a good captain down here and then you make him inspector and we lose him."

The point is this: The territorial imperative develops a family feeling in the people who are a part of the territory. It isn't just the head lion; it is the lion cubs and the female lions and all the other lions. They are saying, "This is our territory. There had better not be any other cats in here trying to take us over. If some stray lions come in here, they are going to get it." Even if the stray lion is bigger and stronger, the lion who is the leader of this turf is probably going to whip the bigger, stronger lion from a different area. It's the concept that every creature has its turf and no one had better violate that creature's turf. You can do it, but you do it at the peril of getting the hell knocked out of you by somebody who is a lot smaller than you are.

If you subjugate those people and they still have that feeling of turf, 50 or 100 or 1,000 or 10,000 years later, they're going to go back and get their turf. That's what the Jewish people have done in Israel, and that's the problem with the Palestinian Arabs who feel they've been dispossessed from Palestine. Englishmen and Scotsmen came into Northern Ireland and took it over, and there's still fighting going on. People are being killed there today because of the territorial imperative. Even though that's a part of Great Britain, it is a desperate problem for the British. There will be no solution to it unless they become different people. There's nothing that is more powerful than the concept of people's being a part of their own turf.

In the organization of a police department, employing the concept and the power of the territorial imperative and its reaction on human being is a very smart way to get a tremendous increase in public cooperation. The impetus that it will give to reducing crime is unequaled; it works. In Chatsworth, where my own family lives, we are sort of country people; some people have horses, and we have a lot of open space. We are different from the Northridge people, who adjoin us only a few miles away. Northridge people are sort of city people living out in the country; they have bigger houses, and they may be fancier and more sophisticated. There is a real difference between us Chatsworth cats and those Northridge cats who live right next to us. So we have the Chatsworth team, which is Team One, and the Northridge team, which is Team Three, and we took advantage of the difference between those teams and the difference in those people. When you carve out these hunks of territory so that the people have as far as possible a geographical or other kind of identity with one another, it makes for a stronger turf. Where factors of a common culture, ethnicity, interests, wealth, or poverty can be put into the mix, it makes for a lot stronger force for good police service.

MANAGEMENT BY PARTICIPATION

A police organization must use and understand the concept of management by participation. To explain this concept very generally, someone—the leader, perhaps—will establish certain agreed-upon objectives or goals. Then the setting of additional goals and subgoals is participated in by people down through the hierarchy of the organization, until eventually, the process involves people at every level. (More will be discussed about goals under "Management by Objectives.") To get the greatest bang for the buck, everyone in the organization should participate in the decision-making process. Everybody down to the lowest practical level who can participate in management decisions should be permitted to do so. Decisions will then be richer, much richer. Such an approach is extremely practical, because the people who are responsible for accomplishing the task are the ones who are best able to tell whether the idea will or won't work.

The opposite of management by participation is authoritarian management, autocratic management, or, simply put, management by the boss. There are serious limitations to that kind of management. If the welfare of the people of the City of Los Angeles had to depend on my thinking of everything that had to be done, my department would not be very effective. You have to be willing to share your role as an executive, as a leader, with a great many people in your organization; to charge them with the responsibility of doing what has to be done.

When you do this, you pay a price. Sometimes your people might do something in a way that you wouldn't have done it. But generally, they are going to do what you would have done if you had the time to do it or think about it. In fact, it's not really a price—it's a benefit, because sharing that authority turns people on. If people in an organization know that they don't have to do anything until the boss tells them to do it, they may not do anything.

Such an organization would operate under the same absurd concept I experienced in the navy, where the boss said, "Dig this ditch three feet deep between these two stakes from here to the corner, and I'll be back about noon. Then I'll tell you what to do next." If the boss gets tied up someplace else, the workers are going to be sitting on the dirt pile telling stories and not digging any ditches.

Management by participation charges people with the responsibility for taking an active part in the setting of goals and for knowing how the job should be done. It has a self-energizing effect on people. They go forward even when there are no further instructions and do what has to be done.[4] It is certainly a more gratifying method of working as a subordi-

---

[4]Rensis Likert, *The Human Organization and Its Management* (New York: McGraw-Hill, 1967).

nate, knowing that you have the discretion to use your judgment within department rules and figuring out not only what to do but how to do it, rather than waiting for someone to tell you what to do. It helps also to know you are going to get backing for it as well!

A classic example of the results of nonparticipation was an experience of mine in the United States Navy during World War II. I was in a stevedoring battalion, all the decisions were made by our commander; the brass didn't believe in management by participation. I was in charge of a slinging crew on the dock, and we were loading some big, heavy 90mm antiaircraft guns into a cargo ship, the U.S.S. *Spika,* which was going up to the Bering Sea from Adak.

We were using four individual wire slings attached to four different corners of these guns and then lifting them with the jumbo boom. Now, light cargo loaded by hand requires two booms with pulleys on them. But these 90mm guns were heavy enough to require the use of the jumbo boom.

Then, the commander, our boss, came along, took a look, and said, "Davis, what's the matter with you? Don't you know there's a war going on? What are you loading those guns with those four slings for? You go get those vehicle spreaders and you put those guns in that ship with those vehicle spreaders."

Well, now, I couldn't very well say, "Commander, I believe in participative management. I have thought this through, sir, and even though it takes a little bit longer to attach the slings with U-bolts, I think the job can be accomplished better this way. Vehicle spreaders are designed to load relatively lightweight six-wheel trucks, and these guns have a lot more metal in them, sir. It's liable to be unsafe, sir." If you said that to our commander, you would end up in the brig

So, when he gave me that speech, I said, "Yes, sir," and had my men bring over the vehicle spreaders. After all, I was a boatswain's mate first class and he was a full commander. A boatswain's mate first class just doesn't tell a commander what to do—at least not in World War II in 1943. He was the big cargo executive. He got his experience in the South loading bales of cotton on ships. My experience in rigging came from being a tree surgeon before I was old enough to be a policeman. My own experience involved moving trees fifty or sixty feet tall and lifting them out of the ground, my experience with cargo was limited. He was the cargo expert.

So we got the vehicle spreaders, the boom came over, the boom picked up the big gun, and we were very tense. We thought, "Maybe this old man knows what he's talking about." The boom got over the hold of the ship and started letting out line. It went down about three feet, and the welded ring that held the vehicle spreader together at the top gave way. That 90mm gun damn near sank the U.S.S. *Spinka.*

That was the way it was in the navy. When we got through with a job, we had to sit and wait for the officers to come and tell us what to do next. They felt because we were enlisted men we were all a bunch of dummies. There were longshoremen and loggers in that outfit. There were steel construction workers who had lifted steel up hundreds of feet in the air and put buildings together. And many of the officers we had in that battalion were jackasses who thought all the knowledge in the world resided in them. We were a great outfit, and we may have done great things, but we didn't do them through management by participation. How much better it would have been for the commander to have allowed me, as an "expert slinger," to put those guns aboard that ship. Fortunately, we never lost a gun. But that slight loading mistake probably cost the United States Navy Navy several hundred thousand dollars because they didn't believe in management by participation.

On another occasion, many outfits had been camped aboard ships in a bay for months and months. Eventually, in a glorious assault, some army, navy, and marine units invaded Kiska. We discovered that there wasn't a single Japanese there. Later, when we were flying back to Anchorage, Alaska, a guy aboard the plane, a navy CPO, said, "I could have told them there were no more Japanese there. I was flying over that thing every day in my PBY.'' He wasn't supposed to have done this, and worse still, he had gone in there and dropped a few bombs just for the hell of it. But he knew there weren't any Japanese there. My outfit stayed on Adak for a long, long time. We held up a lot of the military resources of the government of the United States because the navy didn't believe in participatory management.

An energized organization that is really on its toes has a deep and strong belief in management by participation. The genius of American industry is that its workers are treated like intelligent human beings. And one of the reasons we have been successful from a military standpoint is that generally, we have more participation in management than most other countries do.

In my college teaching days many years ago, there were usually a few students from other countries in my classes. One of my students was a sergeant from the young state of Israel. In my classes we spent a great deal of time on management by participation, even 20 years ago. The sergeant took me aside at one of the coffee breaks and said, ''Let me guarantee you that I'm not going to use any of your stuff in Israel, because there the boss makes the decisions. The captain makes the decision and the lieutenant carries it on.'' Thinking back now, considering the way they handled the Six-Day War, they must have learned something about management by participation. If they hadn't, they would have been dead waiting for people to decide what was going to happen when the Arabs attacked.

I can recall an example of how I applied MBP as a police lieutenant. It was during an assignment to our Newton division, which became my favorite division of the LAPD. I had just finished an assignment writing the department manual. (I was considered a bookworm at that time, even though I had spent seven years on the street as a policeman. But my most recent assignments as a sergeant were in staff jobs, so I was branded.) The captain called me in and said, ''Lieutenant, I have no doubt that you are the most qualified

142

officer on the Los Angeles Police Department—academically,'' which meant he didn't think I knew a damn thing about police work.

It figured that if the captain felt that way, the men felt that way. So I tried to define what the most critical problem was on my watch, the nightwatch. (This was long before team policing or anything like it.) I saw from the crime reports that the burglary problem was mainly in a certain place at a certain time. The burglars were attacking windows off alleys. Simple enough, you might think; just tell the men what to do and the problem will be solved. But that was not what I did. It was smarter to talk to my watch and say, ''This is what seems to be the nature of our burglary problem. We've got more burglaries here, and they are happening in this way.'' And then I asked, ''How are *we* going to do it? How are *we* going to catch these burglars?'' In a way, my question surprised them. But it made sense. Letting those policemen participate in deciding how we were going to go about it produced a better solution than anything I could have come up with. They were absolutely superb! Once they saw the objective, they accomplished the mission. They knew the things that didn't work and the things that did. They went out and did a tremendous job for me.

And they made me look good to that captain. When I transferred out of there a year later, that same captain gave me the highest rating I had ever had up until that time. His comments on how much I knew about police work and what a great policeman I was were the capper. The great policemen were, of course, my sergeants and my men, particularly the policemen.

I hadn't made the same mistake that the navy commander had made. So my advice to those people who are telling their subordinates to ''get those vehicle spreaders'' is that they ought to be saying, ''Hey, fellows, you see these 90mm guns? We've got to get them down in the hold of that ship.'' If the men know their business, they are going to get them down there better and faster and safer than you can tell them how to do it. That is management by participation.

MANAGEMENT BY OBJECTIVES

Managing by objectives is something that every executive should become familiar with. It is a whole management style in which superior and subordinate jointly identify common goals, define responsibilities, and use these as guides for assessing performance effectiveness. Employees participate by the interaction of setting their own goals, and a great deal can be accomplished to promote understanding of specific organizational goals.

There is an interesting exercise for managers who want to better understand management by objectives. You may have done it yourself. People within a working environment should be asked what they think they are supposed to be doing for a living. Most managers will be amazed—even shocked—at some of the responses.

I conducted this exercise years ago, as a lieutenant. First, each of my six field supervisors, my sergeants, was asked, "What does each of you do for a living?" The responses indicated, after all was said and done, that each sergeant was doing *my* job. They were in charge of everything on that watch. So I had them all come in together and said, "It is obvious that something that everybody does, nobody does; and each of you has told me that you supervise every man, all 50 men on this watch. I thought *I* was doing that."

Next, I proposed a plan to divide the work so that errors would not be made in someone else's area of responsibility. Each one of them was assigned three or four cars and given specific responsibility for the officers on those cars. They were told that these were going to be their cars for the month and they were responsible for the quantity and the quality of work the officers under their command produced. Then we put up a pin map displaying these contiguous districts, and we put a flag on each area with the name of the sergeant in charge of it.

One sergeant, who didn't think much of my idea, said, "You are not going to put your work off on me. I have always worked for a strong leader, and you are a weak leader. You are trying to delegate your responsibility to your subordinates." He immediately transferred out of the division on his own.

Once those individual sergeants were held responsible, I got a much better performance from my people. Through the application of management by objectives, we were talking about burglaries and robberies and other problems on the watch among ourselves. The job was getting done, and everyone knew what the problems were. But when everyone thought that they were doing everyone else's work, no one had any responsibility at all.

Such an exercise might be interesting for others to try. Figure out for yourself what people are supposed to be doing. Then call them in and ask them what they are supposed to be doing. It may be that there is very little congruence between what the leader thinks his people are supposed to be doing and what they think they are supposed to be doing. If that is true, management by objectives may be an answer.

Before an executive begins to install a system of management by objectives, people should be made to understand their roles in the organization, so that they can more realistically define problem areas. If no one really knows what his duties are, goals cannot be established. After roles and areas of responsibility are established, both manager and subordinate can sit down and develop a realistic statement of goals to be achieved.

The entire system of MBO and reasonable methods of using this technique are described in several management books. But here, briefly, is the step-by-step process:

1. Near the end of the budget year, the manager should review available information and come up with a brief statement reflecting very broad goals for the coming year, such as "a reduction in crime."

2. The subordinates should then be asked to evaluate the statement and come up with a specific goal, for example, "a reduction of crime by 10 percent."

145

3. The goal should then be reviewed jointly to make sure that it is both attainable and challenging. Both might then decide how the goal will be met.

4. The goal, once established, should be incorporated into the budget. Goals should not be fixed in cement, but should be flexible enough to permit changes in the state of things that are beyond the subordinate's control; e.g., a flood or serious economic crisis.

5. Some form of follow-up may be needed to reinforce the goal process during the period in question. Periodic discussions may be profitable to provide guidance if that is necessary.

6. At the conclusion of the goal period, or at regular intervals if the goals are applied to ongoing objectives, objectives should be reviewed for the purpose of making performance evaluations.

When installing any system of MBO, managers would be well advised to take a look at the experiences of other organizations. Unrealistic goals or a shortcutting of the process might result in a disaster for the organization. The leader cannot be a prisoner of his subordinates under this system, and the subordinates should not be placed in a position where they are operating without management backing.

An MBO system will not work well if management attention is lacking. Likewise, it will falter if it is applied only at one or two levels within the organization. The burden must be borne proportionately by all levels.

12
Command Control

As we saw in the preceding chapter, participative management can solve many organizational problems. But at the same time, a centralized control—the core of the organizational sphere—is necessary in police work as in other types of organizations. It is the means by which we gain an overall view of the conditions under which the agency must work, through the accumulation of information about crime in the community.

The material that follows illustrates the necessity for such command control.

PROACTIVE POLICE WORK

Crime

A crime occurs, the police are called, they catch or attempt to catch the suspect, and perhaps they take him to court. It's all a very time-consuming, slow, laborious method of getting police work done. That is why the best police work anticipates what is going to happen, predicts where it is going to happen, and deploys to intercede and prevent it from happening. Thus, the best form of police work is proactive police work, thwarting the commission of a crime or a breach of the public order—whether it is a burglary or a bombing, or whatever it happens to be.

Traffic accident prevention is a good example. If the presence of uniformed policemen will make people drive within the law and if that's going to make it safer, then that's a lot better than hiding behind a sign or a tree and racing out from behind it to stop someone who went through a signal. It is a little late by then. It would be much more productive to be proactive and prevent the violation in the first place than to be reactive and merely cope with the consequences of the unlawful act.

What this requires, of course, is gathering data beforehand that will tell what has been happening, simultaneously gathering information about who is doing it, and, by whatever legal sources are available, finding out what the bad guys are planning to do. In the area of gathering public-disorder intelligence information, for example, about those deluded people who want to bomb radio stations or police stations, the idea would be to know in advance what the bomber is going to do and then to thwart the activity. Likewise, if we find out that 15-year-old Johnny Smith is a burglar and that he is on dope, which means that he is surely going to steal to support his dope habit, then it is a lot more productive to figure out where Johnny Smith is going to be and get him as soon as he attempts some crime, thus thwarting his activity rather than waiting for the crime to occur and looking for him then.

In Los Angeles, we have one division that keeps tabs on the really bad guys. The officers identify a particular bad guy, they find out where he lives, and they watch him, all day if necessary. If he is seen going into an apartment house and coming out with something in his hands, he is theirs. First we look for a victim, and when we find a victim, we snap up the burglar. There are some people who make their living by throwing bombs or burglarizing, or by some other kind of criminal activity. Some people forget that. If we merely respond to the crime, take a report, and then try to put it together academically after it has all happened, we are only being reactive. We are going to be very ineffective if that is all we do. The only way to reduce crime is to be proactive as well.

You can have proactive police work with burglars, proactive police work with stick-up men, proactive police work with a great percentage of crimes—but, of course, not all. Many crimes happen spontaneously, without any pattern. There is nothing much you can do about it. But law enforcement agencies have an obligation to spend a maximum amount of time on proactive police work, not reactive police work. Any dummy can go out and take a report. It takes someone with a little bit of interest and imagination to figure out what's going to happen in advance and to take steps to prevent it or minimize the damage.

Law enforcement has computer systems that can put together *modus operandi* information from the past to predict where you should deploy your forces by hour of the day, by day of the week, by type of crime, and by a great many other factors. In Los Angeles, we have a computer system called PATRIC that helps solve crimes. It also attempts to predict areas in which crimes are apt to happen, based upon what has happened in the past. That is a sort of abstraction of the concept of being proactive. Where you are dealing with an actual individual or organization, and you find that, let us say, they are planning to execute someone and you learn how they are planning to do it, then you can really be proactive rather than reactive.

Traffic

It is surprising that traffic, the part of police work that seems to have the least appeal to most policemen, has been the most proactive of all police work. In the late thirties, traffic professionals in American policing, together with the people in the insurance industry who were most concerned about the problem, put together a course of training and a philosophy of preventive enforcement or selective enforcement at Northwestern University. Essentially, it was a proactive, preventive sort of thing designed to reduce traffic accidents. Nobody wants to go in after somebody gets killed in a traffic accident and then find out what happened. We apply what we learn from previous accidents—where they happen, when they are happening, the kinds of people that are involved—but then we go out to enforce the appropriate law and try to prevent future accidents from happening.

Los Angeles put in that system on March 17, 1941.[1] I was assigned to the newly created Traffic Bureau of the Los Angeles Police Department. We had three weeks of intensive training in all aspects of selective enforcement. Traffic accidents had been killing 500 people a year back then. Within a few years, through selective enforcement and prevention and engineering and education and all the other factors that went into the program, we had cut traffic deaths in half. Today, by a continuous application of those same principles plus some new techniques, and even though the population of the city has gone up tremendously and the number of cars has increased astronomically, we kill fewer people a year in traffic accidents than we did 35 years ago.

International Association of Chiefs of Police, *Selective Traffic Enforcement Manual* (Washington, D.C.: International Association of Chiefs of Police, 1972).

Each year during my tenure as chief, the LAPD has received a national award for the reduction in fatalities in our city. One of our major objectives has been reducing traffic accidents. My officers try everything we old-timers did, but then they use their imagination and go beyond what we did. They think, for example, "A lot of accidents today involve bicyclists, so we have to get at the bicycling population. We have to give some selective enforcement to bicycles." So now they write some tickets for dangerous bicycle violations. You know that no policeman likes to write a ticket for a kid riding a bicycle! But it might save the kid's life.

One of my deputy chiefs found that a great many traffic fatalities involve motorcyclists. California is one of the two states that doesn't require a helmet for motorcyclists. So this chief had his men stop every non-helmeted motorcycle rider and give him a polite little lecture about wearing a helmet. When it was over, most of them would say, "Thank you." The Hell's Angeles and some of the other motorcycle people in California had a big demonstration not long ago to prevent the state from requiring them to wear helmets. Yet even though there is no law requiring it, we try to talk people into doing it to keep them alive.

We found also that a great many of the victims of traffic fatalities were young children who had run out into the street. This same innovative deputy chief established a "Save-a-Child Program." If a toddler runs into the street, a big uniformed policeman grabs this little kid and says, "Take me to your leader." When he finds the mother, all three of them— the mother, the little kid, and the uniformed policeman—sit down together and have a little chat about kids getting killed by automobiles.

Programs like this have resulted in a reduction in traffic-related deaths of little children and motorcyclists. That's proactive police work. We could just wait and let the little kids get run over and then send the bodies to the morgue; that's reactive. When we get the little kids before they get hit and talk to them and their mothers, that's proactive.

The parent has more control over the child than a policeman does. The policeman is limited by the fact that he can't stay there and watch over the kid, but he can be the catalyst to save the kid's life. If parents are approached properly, most of them are responsive. If they are not, there is nothing much you can do. There are some things we can't change. God gave us the will to try to change people, but he also gave us the wisdom not to waste our time trying to convince people who will not be convinced.

Disasters

Another example of proactive police work involves planning for major unusual occurrences. Several years ago, I had to make a decision about the Bel-Air section of Los Angeles. I was an inspector then, and the Santa Monica mountains were a part of my overall area of responsibility. There was this huge spread of California sagebrush and mesquite before me. I thought, "Boy, some day this is going to go!" So we did some planning. I had all my captains conduct command-post exercises.

First, we had to ask ourselves, "What is our legal obligation on evacuation?" Under California law, the fire chief is given great power in evacuating buildings or whole blocks and blowing them up. Whatever he has to do to stop a fire, he can do. The police also have the power to evacuate if there is danger of loss of life. We made a decision, and we put it in the department's training bulletins, that we were not going to waste our time arguing with people who don't want to be saved. We would lose the precious time we needed to get to those who did want to be saved. Officers were told to try to convince people quickly that they should evacuate. If they wouldn't leave, the officers were to go on. Perhaps those people were going to burn to death, but it would be a result of their own personal judgment. At least we could get to three or four other people who wanted to be evacuated.

It is hard to imagine a California brush fire unless you

have seen one. The brush is ten or fifteen feet tall, and some of the houses are built right next to it. The brush gets very, very dry. When we did, unfortunately, experience that huge brush fire, 400 homes burned absolutely to cinders. It was a horrendous conflagration. But we went through that whole holocaust with not one human life lost, because our effort was proactive, not reactive.

Another year a reservoir broke through, and we lost a lot of people; we hadn't planned for such a disaster. But now, every year, we review our plans. We know all the terrain of the city; every district has topographical maps. We can tell what part of the city might be inundated if any damn breaks. We will be prepared to assist in the evacuation of any portion of the city.

In 1971, we had to evacuate a part of Los Angeles after the earthquake. Some 80,000 people were evacuated from their homes. There was the very real danger of a dam breaking, but once we got the Army Corps of Engineers in to help pump it out, the problem was alleviated. Then Whoever was shaking the earth stopped, and those people were able to move back into their homes. Our efforts had been successful. That was proactive police work.

Until the leader makes the transition in his thinking from reactive to proactive, his working day will be spent running from one crisis to another. If he puts off being proactive long enough, he may work his way to an early grave or, if he is lucky, an early retirement. Not a very pleasant way to go.

VICE CONTROL

The enforcement of the vice laws also requires very sensitive command control. It is a matter of management vigilance, both internally and externally.

Individual vice officers, after a few months in vice work, consider themselves to be real geniuses and great masters of the mysteries of this shady world. Many of them believe that only they know how to work a prostitute or bookmaker or lottery scheme. They believe they have informants who come just to them because they have some mysterious charm. Of course, all of that is baloney. Most informants are interested in either getting money as payment for their tale, or continuing an illegal enterprise, or getting off for something they have done. That same informant will go up to *any* man on the police department and provide the same information, if it is worth it to *him*. That doesn't change the fact that effective vice-law enforcement is based upon sound information. The one and only reason the police get that information is very simple. It is a case of one businessman wanting to dominate his competition. If one businessman can sabotage his fellow businessmen and remain unsabotaged himself, he will make more money. One gambler, one whore, whatever, will very willingly act as an informant to hurt somebody else so that he or she can make more money. That is why vice-law enforcement has so many informants. And that is why it is so important to have sensitive administrative control: to see to it that nobody goes free.

There are often so many tricks on the street who have designs on the local women that a decent woman cannot wait for a bus without being propositioned. We have arrested doctors, lawyers, and even a police official. The policeman was prosecuted right along with everyone else.

Male solicitors of prostitution are arrested with a great deal of regularity in my city. If there is any credibility to the stories presented in magazines and books with regard to current sexual openness and the availability of sexual partners, then sexual participation with a prostitute is a sad commentary on American manhood. Perhaps the prostitute's customers cannot communicate in a nonsexual manner, or perhaps we just have a bunch of tongue-tied males who are afraid to talk to women and afraid of themselves. Well, that just means more women for the normal, well-adjusted male suitor.

Bookmaking investigations have to be handled differently from prostitution investigations. When I was a captain, there was a certain "Mr. Big bookmaker who had some fifteen agents working for him. These agents worked, at that time, for about $65 to $70 a week, and he paid their expenses if they got arrested. They kept no records. When the phone rang, they gave their bets to the gal in the relay office. She, in turn, was called by a back office. All the papers recording various bets were destroyed along the way, so there was no day-to-day record of all the activity, except in the back office. And one man was at the top—Mr. Big!

We found that Mr. Big's fifteen agent books were seldom arrested. Everyone else was falling, but Mr. Big was the biggest guy and he was getting away clean.

We were putting together intelligence at that time on bookmakers and their agents. My men were forgetting to nail Mr. Big's agents, not because the officers were crooked or because they were taking payoffs; they were passing his men by because he was giving them information on all the other bookmakers. He was a great informant, and the policemen were letting him, one of the biggest bookmakers in town, run his business without fear of arrest because they were able to clean up the rest of the division with his help. After we finished with the competition, I told my vice officers they would have to get another informant in order to get the goods on the big man. In a period of less than three years, we went from 144 cash rooms to four, and those four were real hard-core joints.

What all this means, then, is that in order to control vice, first the police must know what vice conditions exist, and that requires intelligence information, which means research. Second, a broad general enforcement policy must exist that precludes anyone from getting a free ride. Regardless of what information an informant gives, it won't keep him from going to jail. Third, conspiracy cases must be put together so that Mr. Big, who cannot be arrested at the street level, is included.

The Mr. Bigs in vice activity work with what they call a long stick. They sit back in their fancy offices or their condominiums and have agents working for them. They make sure that records that will lead to them are not kept. Investigations leading to the big man require ingenuity and a great deal of investigative work. A successful prosecution under the conspiracy statutes is difficult, but it is worth it. A conspiracy case is the only way to take Mr. Big and break his racket. It is absolutely unfair to just knock off the street-level agents. In fact, it is un-American! Unless we are going to get to the roots of the devil grass, we won't really clean the weed patch. And unless we can create fear that we are going to get to those roots, there is a very real danger that we will have *de facto* legalized vice.

Vice work is too important and too demanding to permit the vice cop, who sees only one aspect of it, to be the only one involved. Vice control is so important in my department that we have two levels of enforcement. We have for some time had people responsible for suppressing vice at the district level, and at another level, an administrative vice squad that works for the chief and determines the broader picture of vice activity. This squad does make an occasional arrest if the need arises, but primarily it gets information on just what the city's vice problems are. One enforcement group is watching another enforcement group. We have that arrangement because there is a great opportunity for corruption in vice work. The purveyor of vice would like nothing better than to pay off policemen in order to guarantee the security and success of his business.

In Los Angeles, we also have an 18-month rotation policy for area vice squads and a three-year rotation policy in our administrative vice division. Once an officer's time is up, we move him out. The officer screams, "How can you get rid of me? I know everything there is to know about this very complicated Chinese gambling thing." How wrong he is! Within three months, we will have some other young officer who will know everything there is to know about complicated Chinese gambling, just as the first officer did after three months—but he has forgotten that. Policemen are highly innovative and they learn quickly. If you leave policemen too long in vice control, it is bound to have a bad effect on them. All they are dealing with is scum and slime, and pretty soon they may think the whole world is that way. That is very unfair to the officer himself; it is unfair also to the people he works with. Experience has shown that when you let an officer stay four and five years, even in the administrative end where there isn't as much hazard, sometimes his view of things becomes distorted. He sees the whole world as a conspiracy. Eighteen months at the divisional level and three years at the administrative level is enough scum and slime for anyone. The next guy who comes into the unit is going to be able to do a better job than the man he is replacing.

Enforcing vice laws has caused some controversy of late. Those who would promote the virtue of vice (please pardon the non sequitur) would have us believe that society has no stake in the enforcement of laws pertaining to private behavior. As with the organized criminal and others, the premise is self-serving and foolish. It is one of several myths that have been promoted by those who appear to place no value on morality.

13

Personnel Management

The subject of personnel management has been the topic of entire volumes. Motivation and direction have been discussed in other parts of this book, but I have made no particular attempt till now to specifically discuss personnel matters.

My comments specifically directed to personnel management are restricted to the decision-making process for selection of personnel for special assignments or elevation to non–civil service positions, which is probably the most politically sensitive subject among policemen—or anyone in an organization; to the subject of women in policing, particularly as it applies to hiring standards for the police service; and to the vital subject of discipline.

SELECTION AND HIRING

The effective manager expends a considerable amount of his time on personnel matters, whether it is in assigning personnel, implementing policy that affects them, or disciplining them. As time passes, more of that time is being spent on matters involving personnel selection and hiring, particulalry with the increasing involvement of the courts and the federal government in local government affairs.

It has been my policy to allow my subordinates to select the people they want and to participate with my assistant chiefs only in the selection of deputy chiefs and in the assignments of Captains III, those who are in charge of a geographical area or district. Occasionally there is a need to override a decision and put my choice into an area, but I usually just participate with the assistant chief in those decisions. In most other cases, the deputy chiefs and I stay out of the process and allow a lieutenant to select his policemen and sergeants, and a captain to select all his people. Other than having to select from a civil service list or from an internal selection pool, middle managers are generally allowed to select their own people.

We do tell them, "Don't be absolutely parochial about it; give somebody outside the team a chance to move." In that setting, they still do a pretty good job. We did find that when there was total territoriality in the selection process, captains wouldn't select anyone for elevation to Policeman III and Policeman II + 1 except the men who worked for them. We had to say, "If you keep doing that and you don't give anyone else a chance, we will have to step in." Now captains and lieutenants look over the candidates from other places. There is still a strong feeling that the local boy should get it, and that is basically good as long as it doesn't exclude everybody else.

COMPENSATION

People in this country probably believe they are spending enough for their law enforcement agencies. However, pay in the police service is usually not based upon an equitable standard. In police work, as in few other categories of employment, the bulk of the workers not only come in at the basic rank but, even if they do excellent work, are going to be at that rank for their entire career—policemen forevermore. If you want to remain a worker, a practitioner, in the police service, you remain a policeman. You can become a detective or an investigator, but in most departments there is still only one category of policeman.

Almost every other professional endeavor has one, two, three, or even four specialist categories, depending upon the job. There are, for all practical purposes, different levels of responsibility within the rank of policeman; many policemen have much more difficult and complex jobs than others. Yet in America, we generally pay every policeman who has been on the job two or three years the same amount of money that we pay experienced veterans, and most agencies even pay every detective the same amount of money. This is typical in American police departments.

Recently, the federal government asked me to chair two national committees, composed of both professional law enforcement officials and lay citizens, which sought to provide standards for my profession. Each was a task-force effort of major importance to the nation, and in each instance the subject of equitable compensation for our nation's policemen received extensive attention.

It is my contention that how we go about it is more important than how much we are paid, although the question of how much is frequently an important issue. In any event, the issues of minimum performance standards and equitable salary standards are tied directly to each other and should always be discussed together.

Police officers are as much entitled to appropriate compensation as are any other workers in society, but the

161

police have not been appropriately paid on a voluntary basis anyplace in this country, or indeed anyplace in the world. Where there has been a great economic dislocation of police compared to the rest of society, it has never been remedied just out of the goodness of the hearts of city fathers or citizens of any city. Our towns' and cities' government officials—and in fact, even police administrators—have failed to ensure an adequate level of compensation for police officers. This neglect would seem to imply that these officials think of policemen as less important than skilled craftsmen such as electricians, plumbers, refrigerator repairmen, and carpenters. If we averaged the wages of all those crafts, we would probably find that all across the nation, fixing an air conditioner, repairing a broken drainpipe, or installing electrical wiring is generally better compensated than the job of keeping a city from being raped, ravaged, and pillaged.

There is something wrong with society's values when dedicated law enforcement officers are in an economically depressed category, forcing their wives to work or forcing the officers themselves to take second jobs—in effect, subtracting from the amount of time they can devote fully to their primary employer. There is nothing good to be said about the level of compensation of police officers in the whole world today, yet it is only because of their dedication that society is safe.

So it would appear that a man has to be some kind of a fool to be a policeman. When you think that his job is one in which he will risk his life any time of the day or night for people he has never seen—people he may not even like, people who may not like him—it must be concluded that such a man is a fool. A very dedicated and much needed fool perhaps, but a fool nonetheless. Instead of taking advantage of that kind of man, society should say, "We are glad that somebody is foolish enough to be a police officer." They should also say, "We must see to it that he is as well compensated as the man we ask to fix our toilets or television sets.

Bases for Compensation

Compensation presents a unique problem to the police service in that it is frequently more complicated than just a matter of granting a salary increase. If 30 percent, say, were simply added to the pay of all those in the present rank structure, a city might then be overpaying a great many people. The problem may revolve more around a lack of adequate differentiations in rank for several kinds of policemen. A great many questions must be asked, particularly about what a policeman does in his work, and where he does it.

There are some duty assignments that by their nature are less desirable than others. In London, for example, the Metropolitan Police have a hard time keeping young men, because housing is harder to find there but the housing allowance isn't any greater. The pay isn't any higher in London, and yet the London "bobby," if he lives out in the suburbs, has to drive an inordinate distance and fight his way through traffic; whereas the country policeman is able to walk or bicycle to work and can raise his kids in a much different atmosphere, away from big-city crime. And yet the Metropolitan London policeman gets the same pay as any other "copper" in England, because that is the way it is done there. There should be a pay differential for working in different areas and in more difficult or less desirable assignments.

Some policeman have much more responsible jobs than others, and those positions should have higher pay. For others, who do not have that much responsibility but still have more than the average policeman, we can apply a different rate of pay. A city would thus be able to give very high pay to the most responsible positions without giving everyone 30 percent across the board, making the solution economically feasible.

If the problem is compounded because there is only one rank of policemen, it is a good bet that there is also a problem with unrecognized levels of responsibility. To solve the pay problem, you first have to define what the underlying problems are.

The Leader's Role

Shortly after becoming chief, I submitted to my city council the outline of what I called the Career Policeman Plan, which I had thought through as a deputy chief. Its hypothesis went something like this: Most well-adjusted people don't really want to be leaders; they merely want to do their thing. If they like being policemen, they will remain policemen. They may like doing police work in areas of higher responsibility, but they still want to remain in the field. They would prefer to get paid for doing police work, rather than lie to an oral board and say that they want to be leaders. Most who do accept promotions in the police service do so because of the status and pay involved. When a man goes home to his family, he can tell them he has accomplished something. He can show his wife more money in the paycheck, he can have all his friends look up to him, and he can let the neighbors know that he is more than just a regular policeman. But sadly, there is no other occupation in the world that is structured as stupidly as a police organization.

When we put together my plan, we decided to have policemen in charge of police cars in every section of the city, 24 hours a day. These men, called Policemen III + 1's, were each placed in charge of a "basic car." (The guy on *Adam 12* with two stripes and a star on his sleeve is a Policeman III + 1.) The senior man on each watch is a Policeman III; he has stripes but no star. A Policeman I is a recruit in the academy; 18 months later, after he completes probation, he automatically becomes a Policeman II. Thus we created four ranks of policeman.

In addition, the LAPD has three ranks of investigator. An Investigator I is paid slightly less than a sergeant, an Investigator II is paid the same as a sergeant, and an Investigator III is paid slightly less than a lieutenant. So we made it possible for a man to go through four ranks of policeman and three ranks of investigator and still be a worker. He can still get his kicks out of being a good police officer, repressing and solving crime without ever having to supervise anyone.

In Joe Wambaugh's books, the supervisors are a bunch of "no-goodniks." No one likes them, and they have all the headaches in the world. Really, it often seems it's a bum racket to be a leader or supervisor. And sometimes it is only the maladjusted who want to supervise and lead. A big problem in running an organization is sorting out the most maladjusted so they don't get into positions of leadership.

As chief, I was able to get my city council's approval for the Jacobs Company to come in and study the problem. Jacobs recommended the structure that we now have (see chart on page 166). As a result, policemen are probably not underpaid in Los Angeles. But it is stupid to pay everybody the same amount of money. The key factor is that as the leader of my organization, I had a responsibility to think out the problems facing my personnel, particularly as to their everyday situation. The leader is the guy who has to do that. Then he must make the case for a change if it is called for.

A system with multiple pay grades within each rank provides an added advantage to the police leaders. It gives managers greater flexibility in the movement of people. In Los Angeles, we give pass-fail written exams for advancement to Policeman III and an oral exam for advancement to Sergeant II and Investigator III; but after that, the selection of personnel is in the hands of those who must lead these people—the lieutenants and captains. Those eligible for advancement are placed in general classification pools, which sort them into Outstanding, Excellent, Satisfactory, and Unsatisfactory categories. Thus, an element of merit selection enters into the traditional civil service structure.

With the management ranks of lieutenant and captain, there is no testing. The decision to place a person in an advanced pay-grade position, such as Lieutenant II or Captain II or III, is within the power of the immediate superior or the chief of police. Thus, in all ranks, some flexibility remains

165

Career Development
Reward for Responsibility

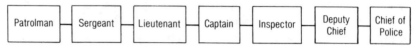

Policeman ⇒ Chief of Police

PAST

PRESENT

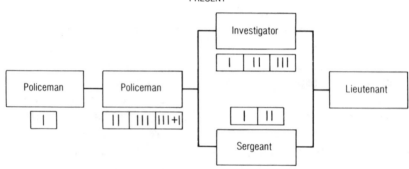

Policeman ⇒ Lieutenant

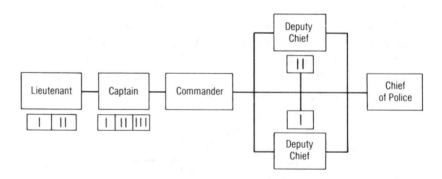

Lieutenant ⇒ Chief of Police

for rewarding outstanding performance. That flexibility is designed to complement an equitable system for assigning personnel with a realistic structure for leading them. Providing that balance is one of the most critical responsibilities of the police leader.

A fellow by the name of Machiavelli said, 500 years ago, that a wise prince takes care of his servants—that if he doesn't, if he is parsimonious in dealing with them, they will have to think about their own well-being and will have to spend their time taking care of themselves instead of the prince. Machiavelli's words held wisdom. A chief executive should see that his subordinates are properly taken care of.

When I was a deputy chief, a friend and neighbor of mine who was associated with a national electronics corporation came to me and asked to look over our communications system to see whether his company could make some kind of proposal to us. He was assigned to a man by the name of Snyder, a veteran of 20 years in the Los Angeles Police Department.

My friend spent a whole day with Snyder, and when I got home that night, I asked him, "Bernie, how did it go?"

He said, "Fine, except that I'm a little upset with you."

I asked, "Didn't they take care of you?"

"No," he said, "that's not the problem. They took good care of me, and *that's* the problem. I am really angry with you. I've heard you complain about being unable to recruit policemen. Well, this fellow Snyder you assigned to show me around has been with you 20 years. He's an absolutely fantastic man. He does excellent work, and it's a disgrace that you are part of an organization that would keep an excellent man like that and never promote him once in 20 years. You don't even deserve to have him." He went on, "If we can find a place for him in our corporation, we're going to take him."

I thought, "Gee, you try to help your friends out and you get insulted." But his comments made an impression.

Interestingly, the private sector seems to understand the

problem clearly. In the natural marketplace for labor in business and industry, there are salary differentials. In the center of a big city, to get a secretary or a file clerk to come downtown, you have to pay more—and that makes sense. The reason you have to pay more is that is costs money to commute into a city. Parking costs are higher; it costs more for lunches; it takes time to travel to and from work; the work area might be undesirable; and there is frequently more pressure. As a result, salaries are generally $50 to $100 per month higher for a clerical person in the middle of New York, for example, than in one of the suburban New Jersey towns.

The same thing should apply to police officers. A policeman may work in an old, depressed neighborhood, where the schools aren't good; so, because the policeman has a young family, he probably lives in the suburbs. He will, of course, have to drive further to work. It will cost him more, and it will take more of his time away from his family. He has to be compensated for that.

The U.S. Civil Service Commission is now looking into this kind of situation on behalf of the federal employees who work in the same classification but in different parts of the country. That is a step in the right direction. It is unrealistic that for working in the bigger, congested cities, with all the problems and extra expenses attendant to it, there shouldn't be any extra compensation.

Over 20 years ago, as a lieutenant representing police officers in my police association, I fought hard for implementation of a salary-setting formula designed by the Griffinhagen Company for Los Angeles police and fire personnel. That formula established a method for determining the prevailing wages in my community, which permitted a realistic way to determine equitable salaries for police officers. Most important, it removed the process from politics. A court suit further settled that issue. As a result, Los Angeles has been fortunate in being able to avoid the dissension and labor strife that has confronted other cities over police salaries. Even though the concept of the prevailing wage is under attack, mostly from politicians, it has provided my city with an ideal environment for bringing equity to police-officer compensation.

WOMEN IN POLICING

Circumstances have dictated that special thinking be applied to women in policing. We have a couple of dozen who were hired under what we called our "Unisex Program;" those women had to meet all the standards and complete all the training required of male officers. After that, they were assigned just as any other officer would be assigned. Interestingly, one of my supervisors who is married to one of our new policewomen told me, "I'm awfully afraid that she's going to get some brutality complaints. She's working over in my old division, and you look at her, she's a very lovely female but she's big enough to handle herself." That woman is a darn good police officer, and the men like to work with her.

Many women wash out in the academy because God didn't make women with the same musculature in the upper body that men have. But those who do finish are qualified to do the job. That is a far cry from the way some other cities have met the demand for more women in policing. Instead of setting standards, a great many towns and cities, under federal pressure to lower standards, simply hired women, schooled them, and thrust them out onto the street.

In Los Angeles, we have had a type of policewoman who hired on to be just that—a policewoman. In fact, Los Angeles was the first city to hire policewomen—back in 1905.[1] Then, they didn't have to undergo the physical demands of recruit training that we require of the new women. Now, some of the older policewomen have been out in the field as sergeants.

[1]National Advisory Commission on Criminal Justice Standards and Goals, *Police* (Washington, D.C.: U.S. Government Printing Office, 1973).

169

They were recycled, so to speak. We promoted our first female lieutenant in 1975 and a second one early in 1976. Both of them are excellent managers.

Common sense required that special efforts be made to ensure the qualifications of these women, both the older, recycled policewomen and the new women. Statistics show that people who assault policemen tend to be taller than the average policeman, and women are smaller than men; on average, about four to five inches shorter and quite a bit lighter. Now, there are many vocations that women can compete in very successfully; there is no reason why a women can't be as effective as a man in medicine and certainly as an attorney. Police work, however, requires a certain amount of strength and endurance, and if you don't have it, you just don't have it, regardless of sex. It is a difficult job, and one must be mentally and physically fit for it.

Granted, we could use more women in the police service, but I have never believed that we should hire them to just satisfy some artificial percentage quota or to yield to some arbitrary federal guideline. Those nameless, faceless federal bureaucrats who make the guidelines and the demands have no responsibility for the performance of the local police department. They probably couldn't qualify as police cadets, let alone as chiefs of police. They wreck police departments. They are the modern Visigoths.

It would be a very sad day if we started turning loose on the streets of our city women who we knew couldn't do the job. The federal government has attempted to deal with this problem by eliminating height standards in some cases. That is not a reasonable approach to the problem; they are experimenting with short people in a vital profession, one where danger is ever present. It is an experiment that may result in some serious injuries or deaths. Can we look forward to the day when we will hire as police officers little tiny fellows, small enough to be able to walk under automobiles? They will make great undercover people because of their size; no one will ever suspect they are cops.

Interestingly, New York, years ago, changed its height standards to attract more Puerto Ricans. What they got were a bunch of short Irishmen. It just can't be done that way. You can't solve problems by changing standards. The federal government has so screwed up this area of hiring that our cities and towns may never be able to recover. It's absolutely absurd. The federal government was created so we could have a national army, diplomacy with foreign nations, a Supreme Court, and a few other things covered in the Constitution. The rest of this stuff about who should be a policeman or a policewoman is none of their damn business. As long as we can, and where I have anything to say about it, the Los Angeles Police Department will maintain its standards and hire people, regardless of color or sex, who are most qualified to give professional service to the people of Los Angeles.

DISCIPLINE

The Need for Discipline

Discipline is necessary to every organization, whether it is an airline or a college; but in a police department, it is the cornerstone that holds the organization up. Police officers have tremendous discretion. They have the power to take liberty away, to use force—including lethal force. Policemen have a very difficult job, as they are frequently told; they are not all Samsons, as they are less frequently told; and they are not totally without fear, something we must never forget.

Because of the discretion they are given, they are sometimes tempted to abuse their power and authority. But if a police department is to be held in extremely high repute, it must be a well-disciplined agency. Those that are not well disciplined are not held in high repute. The prestige of an individual officer will be pretty much proportionate to the

171

level of discipline in his organization. Discipline here does not refer only to the use of harsh negative treatment that is generally associated with the term. What discipline means is an absolutely honest intent on the part of the police administrator to find all the facts of a particular situation and to give it an objective evaluation. At that point, the good leader applies whatever small or great discipline is necessary to change the behavior in question. Organizational discipline must be personalized, much as criminal justice discipline should be personalized to the criminal; the first offender should be treated more gently than the repeater. And not only should the penalties be progressively harsher for the repeated infractions, but they should be greater for more serious offenses.

In a police agency, if an employee is a threat to the community and we have not learned that at his first disciplinary incident, we can only hope that the second incident will not be serious. If the offense is serious enough, immediate termination may be in order. The increase in penalty is designed to eventually cut out that cancerous part of our profession and eliminate it completely. A constant weeding-out process is necessary to a police agency if it is to remain honest and good to the people it serves.

Where a penalty is assessed in my own department, it is based upon a theory of increasing severity with each similar infraction. When the penalty is increased each time a violation occurs, very serious problems can be prevented. Primarily, such a method deters bad conduct. For instance, as long as I have been on the police department, a failure to complete your firearms qualification during a qualification period has resulted in some penalty. No excuse is permitted for this failure, including sickness and court appearances. An officer has a whole month to qualify in, and if he cannot accomplish it, the fault is his. You can dream up the biggest excuse in the world and it will never mean anything to the LAPD except, of course, if you are away sick or injured for an entire month. Once, after about six months on the job, I forgot to shoot; I had a very good excuse, but it did me no good. I do not believe that I have ever received a second penalty for failing to qualify. I doubt if any member of the department has failed more than four times to shoot during my 30-year career here, because the penalty keeps going up. With a whole month to make qualification standards, an officer must qualify. That is all there is to it, and there is no getting out of it. This same philosophy applies to any other conduct situation.

Citizen Complaints

There must be a method for citizens to make a complaint against a police officer, and every complaint should be investigated in some manner, although many policemen have difficulty understanding this concept. Before I made chief, my department would not take so-called second-party complaints. We changed that soon after I was appointed. If a wife comes into the police station and says that her husband was abused by the police, a report should be made and the complaint should be investigated. An investigator should talk to the husband. Or let's say that some uninvolved party saw a policeman accepting a bribe from someone. The fact that the complaint came from a second or third party would not mean a damn thing to me. We are interested in determining whether or not we have a corrupt policeman. Refusing to take such complaints, insisting that the aggrieved party make the complaint, just isn't practical.

A complaint should be taken from anyone having a basis for complaint. It should be investigated thoroughly, with due consideration for the dignity of the police officer. That is the only way to do it, because if only certain kinds of complaints are accepted, then the agency is just liable to miss the kind of information needed to keep it clean and honest.

Personnel complaints must be investigated at least as thoroughly as serious felony cases. For that reason, my depart-

173

ment tries to utilize as many general criminal investigators in its Internal Affairs Division as it can, rather than using some guy who wants to make a name for himself climbing over the broken bodies of policemen who have erred so he can be chief someday. If anyone believes that he is assigned to internal investigations for the sole purpose of "getting" policemen, his services are not needed as an investigator. The philosophy of internal investigations must be directed at objectively analyzing the facts of a case in an effort to determine if a member of the department is guilty of misconduct or some criminal offense. A biased investigator cannot be objective, and we don't need that kind of man doing internal investigative work. We want the kind of a guy who, if he is investigating robberies or homicides, can say, "This guy did not do it, I am going to turn him loose and apologize to him." That is the kind of man we want doing internal affairs investigations.

The overzealous investigator loses his sense of objectivity and can ruin a police department. We have, over my several years, tried to bring in good, well-balanced types and rotate them through the internal affairs function every two years, because in the past there were some people who seemed to lick their chops when they saw a complaint come in. Obviously, that kind of spirit in an internal investigative operation would do nothing but provide a distorted type of reporting and cause serious morale problems. Internal affairs investigators are rotated just like vice cops. If they were not rotated after about two years of seeing only complaints against policemen and seeing a few bad cops, pretty soon they would begin to believe that all cops are bad. The police service doesn't need that.

In regard to complaints themselves, we initiated a system that protects both the officer and the citizen making the complaint. When a complainant institutes action against an officer and we have only the complainant's word against that of the officer, truly a one-on-one situation, it is always difficult to find out the truth of the matter. But if the story is implausible, we ask the complainant to take a lie detector test to establish his or her veracity. If the complainant agrees to the test, and if he comes out as a darn liar, we don't even talk to the officer. But when the complainant comes out telling the truth, then we offer the officer the same opportunity. We can command him to go on the "monster" if we want to. If the polygraph experts, two or three of them, agree that there is no question but that the complainant is telling the truth, then we'll require the policeman to go on the machine.

For example, we had one case involving a black prostitute with a "rap sheet" containing 50 arrests, who alleged that one of my young black policemen had made a deal with her to engage in an act of prostitution for ten bucks. She said that after they had engaged in the act, he took his gun out of his coat pocket and held the gun on her while he took the ten dollars back. Now, that is a very implausible story. Here is a prostitute with 50 arrests accusing a policeman who had been very thoroughly investigated before coming on the police department, and who had a perfect background, saying that he would pull a gun to rob a prostitute of ten dollars after he had just engaged in an act of fornication. Highly illogical, isn't it? The investigative staff came to me and said, "We are going to have to throw this one away, because she is a whore with 50 priors. The officer tells his story straight, and it's a tie. We can't come up with anything to prove or disprove it." I told them that this whore could be telling the truth, as implausible as it sounded.

The prostitute was asked to go on the lie detector, and she agreed. She was a good subject on the polygraph. She came out as being absolutely truthful. The young officer was called and asked about going on the polygraph because of the prostitute's allegations and her truthfulness in the matter. The officer requested some resignation forms in lieu of the monster. He took a resignation blank, signed it, and that was the last we saw of him.

So the prostitute was telling the truth. And the machine has saved us on many other occasions where we would have been at an impasse.

Now, the use of polygraph information should be restricted administratively. It is necessary to have a two-track system of investigation because when a policeman is accused of violating the law, as with the example where the prostitute alleged the crime of robbery, the officer may be prosecuted criminally. At one time, the whole complaint process was handled as a single investigation, but we learned that an internal investigation might jeopardize a criminal investigation, so now they are separated. Since we do obtain felony complaints against policemen who are suspected of robbery, one investigation must not obtain facts from the results of the other investigation. The officer must be processed through our internal disciplinary machinery, through an administrative tribunal, called a *board of rights,* before he can be terminated. While I have the right to order one of my men to take a lie detector test for administrative purposes, I cannot require him to violate his Fifth Amendment rights against self-incrimination. So the officer must be investigated from a criminal standpoint by robbery investigators, and investigated from an administrative standpoint by internal affairs investigators, and the two sides may never talk to one another.

If we established the robbery, we would go to the district attorney to get a criminal indictment or complaint. The results of the lie detector obtained as a result of the administrative investigation would not be used, because the officer had been forced to give a statement through administrative coercion. We can use that administrative coercion effectively before an administrative tribunal in an effort to get the robber removed from the police service, but we cannot use it criminally against him. This two-track system is an important part of law.

In Los Angeles, we routinely process anything that is a crime through either the district attorney or the city attorney. There was a time when we said that administrative discipline was tough enough, but that changed years ago. Our officers know they are supposed to have a reverence for the law, and if they commit a felony, they are going to be filed on for a felony in addition to being fired. The day is long since gone when one proceeding took care of the other, and we don't need any stickup men or thieves in the police ranks in America.

Preventing Complaints

Discipline must be viewed positively as well as negatively. In a negative way, we can conclude that if we have some rotten apples, it is best to throw them out before they ruin the whole barrel. But we have to look at it in a positive way and conclude that we want to save some people who foul up, because they are not bad. They may embarrass us, but that is a behavior problem and it should be corrected through training and discipline.

About four years ago, we started looking at the policemen who had lengthy disciplinary records. Their records might say, "Conduct Unbecoming an Officer—UNFOUNDED; Excessive Force—UNFOUNDED; Neglect of Duty, or something else—UNFOUNDED." We would look at their partners, the guys who had been working with them, and they would have no complaints. We would think, "This guy has done something serious enough where we are going to have to fire him; if we could have caught him early enough, we might have saved him."

As a result, we started a process where we record the disposition of all complaints on a card. Each officer has a card. If there is a pattern, the card is sent to the officer's captain. We instructed all captains that they were responsible for counseling these policemen. The counsel sessions work like this: "Jim, you are not in trouble, so just relax. Internal Affairs Division sent us your complaint card; you have about a half dozen serious charges that have been lodged against

177

you during your career. On some of the charges, you were exonerated, and some of them were not sustained, but the guys you work with all do good police work and most of them have clean records. What we are after, Jim, is to figure out what it is that you're doing. Perhaps it is the way you are handling people that has given rise to so many complaints. We want to eliminate this problem so you can stay here for your full 25 or 30 years and not get fired, not get suspended, not lose any of your pay, and not be disgraced." Then someone sits down with him in a nondirective interviewing session and tries to give him some insights into what he might be doing. The officer provides some insight into what he is doing, and he may be called back for another session.

We have cut drastically the number of complaints lodged against Los Angeles police officers. The first year it was in effect, we had a 32 percent reduction in complaints. Then we had a 20 percent reduction. As of now, we have about a 50 percent reduction in the number of complaints received against Los Angeles police officers from outside sources when compared with the number of complaints seven years ago. The counseling program is one of the principal reasons for this success, because it prevents a guy from continuing to do the things that prompt a complaint.

I have seen policemen who somebody could have taken aside and talked to, policemen we might have saved. We could have saved them a lot of trouble and we might have saved the department a lot of trouble. Yet few partners ever want to say, "Hey, sit down, partner, I want to straighten you out. You are screwing up out there." Most policemen just want to get away from that kind of guy. He is an accident on its way to happening, and you do not want the accident to happen while you are with him. You would try to tell the lieutenant you wanted to work with old Joe Jones, but you would never tell him what was wrong with Jim Smith. I am not sure you can ask partners to do that anyway. You cannot expect a man to invade the personal mind and thoughts of his partner and straighten him out. The solution is really more of a management responsibility. So we developed our system of counseling.

The program outlined here is a program of positive prevention. What occurred to me was, if we try to prevent crime, why shouldn't we try to prevent misconduct on the part of police officers? We should try to prevent it before the guy puts himself in peril of being terminated. The program is a success; it has reduced complaints and saved the city both embarrassment and replacement costs, to say nothing of the potential problems it saved the community.

A related problem that should be discussed here concerns the huge civil suits being filed against police officers. They are much like the malpractice suits being filed against doctors. This problem is occurring all over the country. It is a national phenomenon, as cities have lost their sovereign immunity that kept people from bringing suits. There has been a gradual growth of these civil suits against policemen primarily because they are very lucrative to lawyers. In lawyers' terms, cities have deep pockets.

A lawyer can get himself a "good" police brutality case, and if he can get it to go to trial instead of a settlement, he gets 50 percent of the judgment. If he gets a half-million dollars for his client, that's a quarter of a million potatoes for himself. Even by the time he cuts it up with his law firm, he has done well. It is a happy hunting ground. There are going to be more civil suits like that. One guy picked up $150,000 in Honolulu and walked out of City Hall saying that he thought it was terrible that the city had to pay; he wanted the police officers who abused him to pay. Well, you can bet there will soon be a day when police officers *will* pay. The courts will assess punitive damages against the officer; in the future, when a city pays off $150,000, another $50,000 in punitive damages will be assessed against the poor copper. He will be paying for the rest of his life. They will grab everything he gets above subsistence, and they will take his home and sell it.

It is critical for those in leadership positions to keep

their men out of trouble. This is one of their primary responsibilities. We don't want any of our men to get in trouble.
We don't want to have to fire any of them. In most cases,
there are early warning signs, providing plenty of opportunity,
if you have the courage, to sit the man down and talk to him
about the problem, in order to prevent him from going so far
that eventually he has to be fired or shackled with a crippling
judgment.

The disciplinary reports used by my department are
somewhat different from most investigative reports. We are
interested not only in the facts of the case, but in whether the
substance of the complaint could have been avoided, and
what the likelihood is of its occurring again.

This view of investigation began with an incident in the
Watts area of my city. It came about after we investigated
this great big fight in Watts where the officers were legally
right. The officers had pulled alongside a car that was double-
parked; they motioned the driver over to the curb and wrote
him a ticket for double-parking in a residential neighborhood.
A fight ensued, and there were injuries on both sides.

Well, the officers were legally right. But—do you normally write a double-parking ticket in a residential neighborhood? A lightly traveled street where traffic could easily pass?
Should they have done it in this case? Probably not. All they
wanted to do was get the car to park at the curb. Why couldn't
they have said, "Hey, you guys. Why don't you pull over to
the curb?" The people in the car undoubtedly would have
pulled over; they might have called the officers a couple of
names, but that would have been it. Writing that ticket caused
a tremendous fight, and numerous man-hours were exhausted
in both the criminal aspects of the case and the internal
investigation.

Each and every personnel complaint is analyzed, whether
the officer was right or wrong, to determine what can be
learned administratively from the matter so that similar
events can be avoided in the future. We learn, for example,
that frequently we get complaints when we are in situations

we should not have become involved with. This generally refers to those petty situations that are really of no serious consequence to the police or to the general public at large. We have found that even though we were legally correct, we have been the losers. All the investigative resources and all the manpower utilized to complete a report costs us something.

The very lodging of a complaint means that somebody has a different view of police conduct. Perhaps that view is negative, and if it is, there is little that can be done to immediately change it. That is why it is important for us to sit down and go over each case in an effort to determine if similar events can be avoided in the future. Administrative insight can provide management with some keys in resolving possible training problems, and it can assist management in correcting behavior that may be legally correct but judgmentally questionable. This insight is a positive product of an otherwise negative function.

14

Problems for
the Police Executive

POLICE CYNICISM

Since 1952, the Los Angeles Police Department has had a psychiatrist examine every candidate who has successfully passed the written and oral examinations. The psychological evaluation is absolutely necessary, because the casualty rate for flipping out due to job pressure is extremely high in police work.

Many but not all police departments give a psychiatric examination; it is my opinion that all would benefit by it. Most departments do take special care to select only the most well-adjusted people to be police officers. Even then, however, many of those well-adjusted young men and women eventually become maladjusted. Instead of continuing to react to other people with some degree of trust and warmth, they slowly begin looking at people with suspicion. Pretty soon, everybody is a bastard. The policeman becomes suspicious of everyone.

Each of us sometimes has the feeling that there are an awful lot of "bad guys" in society. In fact, we may sometimes believe that most people are pretty bad. Police officers have certainly experienced this feeling. It would be surprising if every police officer hasn't felt that way at one time or another; there would be something wrong with him if he didn't. Policemen are human, and they deal almost exclusively with criminals.

Here is what constant contact with bad people does to you. While talking to victims, you think, "My God, look at that wound," or, "What that poor woman who was raped must be going through," or, "This poor child who was murdered who could have been mine." It's a logical next step to say, "The victim and his or her friends or parents are suffering far too much because of this rotten criminal." And pretty soon, the conclusion is reached that, since this type of thing goes on all the time, there are very few decent people around, that the rest of the world is made of up of a bunch of so-and-so's.

Several years ago, a New York City policeman named Niederhoffer, who eventually retired at the rank of captain, wrote compellingly about what happend to a policeman after years of viewing the negative aspects of society.[1] Niederhoffer had degrees as both a doctor of law and a doctor of sociology. His book was, in my own opinion, totally and absolutely valid. He explained the reason for this growth of suspicion and cynicism, and it was really quite simple. When you take an exceptionally well-adjusted person, much more so than average, and subject him to police work, where he has one

[1]Arthur Niederhoffer, *Behind the Shield: The Police in Urban Society* (New York: Doubleday, 1969).

negative contact after another, something happens to him psychologically. He goes out on the street to do his job and sees things. One call might be a family fight. What he sees isn't a family getting along or a family playing together or praying together or working together. It is a family drunk and fighting and cursing. Next, the officer might respond to a robbery call. He gets the suspect, but the suspect is the most miserable, rotten, nasty little snake that he has ever seen in his life.

Thus he goes from one contact with a low-life to another equally scurrilous. His real-life visions are not pleasant, they are disgusting. Most of his contacts involve people who call him because their human nature has let them down. Over a period of days and over a period of months and over a period of years, he is exposed to nothing but the most unpleasant aspects of his fellow man. Based on this kind of exposure to human beings, if he did not conclude that the people he meets were no damn good, there would actually be something wrong with him. He would have to have his head examined.

With all those negative contacts, he is bound to change. The process demands it. It is very much like Pavlov's theory of conditioned response. Pavlov found that he could show a dog some food and get saliva to run from his mouth. Then Pavlov rang a bell when he showed the dog food. Pretty soon the dog began to salivate every time he heard the bell, whether or not there was any food. Pavlov had transferred the response from one thing, the food cup, to another, the bell. This same transfer of response can occur in most human beings. There is a certain conditioned response in law enforcement. If nearly every human being a policeman runs into is a no-good so-and-so, eventually the policeman concludes, with some degree of logic, that *everyone* is a no-good so-and-so. He becomes sour and cynical, and he appears to change. His family believes he has changed, his neighbors believe he has changed, and the people he went to school with logically and naturally believe he has changed.

Some people are smart enough to keep up the kind of

associations that made them what they were in the first place. If those associations were family, church, fraternal organizations, and athletic groups, they can continue their normal relationships with other people—that is, people outside the police world. But that isn't always the case for cops.

One of the biggest problems that a police administrator is faced with is how to keep excellent, fine, exceptionally well-balanced young people, who have come on the department with a great outlook, from becoming a bunch of cynical, paranoid, bitter, not-so-young men and women. If policemen were sent out to see only good people, then they might perceive that the whole world is good. Since that is an unrealistic prospect, we have to look to some other solution.

The solution to police cynicism is very simple. Let's go back to Pavlov for a minute. If ringing the bell means that there is something good, this becomes a conditioned response. If the approach of a human being causes the policeman to think, "so-and-so," that has become a conditioned response. The solution is to set up conditioned responses that are positive in nature. The British police principle that the people are the police and the police are the people, and that they must work together to make a safe community, implies that there are good people. We have to get back to having policemen, who are out there all the time with the bad guys, sit down with the nice guys. That means the average uniformed copper has to meet with the good people.

That was one of the primary purposes of our Basic-Car Plan. The whole idea involved assigning policemen to specific districts and requiring them to have certain positive contacts with the people in their particular district. Each policeman gets to know his people, and it makes a heck of a difference in the nature of those policemen. Not only does it help cut crime and hold it down because of all of the community partners the policeman has, but the policeman himself remains a human being instead of becoming a psychological wreck.

That is one way, in the work situation, to "program in" positive constructive experiences. Another process for creating this positive conditioned response is to get policemen involved in normal civilian relationships—to get them involved in their fraternal orders, to get them involved in their churches, to get them involved in civic groups. Some of the best relationships that have been developed by many of our people have been through membership in service clubs like the Rotary.

PROFESSIONAL SOLITUDE

When you become a top executive, you find that to a great extent you are alone in the world. First, you cannot talk about the problems of your city and your department with other chiefs on a confidential basis. Everyone else can go out and sit in a bar and have a beer and gripe about their boss. The captains in a police department can get together and gripe about the deputy chief, the deputy chiefs can get together and gripe about the chief; but the one guy who is alone, who cannot go cry on somebody's shoulder, is the chief executive. He cannot go to the mayor or to the city council or to the chamber of commerce and complain.

So one of the conditions of being the top executive of a police agency, or almost any other agency, is "professional solitude." A gossipy sort of a fellow, who has to get his strength from constantly hashing over his problems with other people, will find he cannot do this in the police chief executive's job. One qualification for selection of a chief is that he can be gregarious, meet with people within the department and outside the department, and can still work absolutely alone on many other occasions. Some problems can be shared with immediate subordinates, some can be shared with the whole department, some can be shared with the city administration, but others have to be incubated within the chief executive and held there until he can come out openly with them. Without this ability, a leader will just not make it.

It is an unusual attribute. Few people have been in that kind of position, but a few reading these words might be some day. It may be the first real quietness and loneliness that you feel in a professional career. Sometimes the quietness and the requirement for holding things inside can be quite brutal and harsh, requiring a great deal of personal strength. It can come as a very big surprise to someone achieving the top-level position in an organization if he has not recognized the need for coping with that condition. But the ability to cope with it can and should be cultivated.

PERSONAL SOLITUDE

Personal solitude is different from professional solitude, and it must be described differently. When your day is programmed from one end to the other and everyone in the world wants to see you and there are all kinds of problems you have to respond to, it is a pretty severe test of your temperament to cope with the job. You can either become rundown and react in knee-jerk fashion to every little problem, or you can each day renew your ability to look calmly and helpfully and objectively at every problem.

There has to be a certain amount of thinking time for anyone who has the kind of onerous responsibilities that a chief of police has. And that applies to a policeman as well. A policeman's job on the street isn't much different from his chief's job. The radio sends a policeman here and then it sends him there, and somebody calls him, and there is some other problem. He does not have a chance to direct his own personal activities in the space of eight or ten hours. When he gets through his watch, he is all tied up in knots. The completion of that tour of duty is his first opportunity to unwind and do something that he wants to do.

Everyone needs some time to think after being constantly bombarded by noises and calls and people. Personally, I have found the best time to think is early in the morning, because most people are still sacked out. Things are quiet early in the morning. The only thing you find up at 5:30 or 6:00 A.M. are the birds. When I run in the morning, all the birds are out in the park raising Cain, shouting that the sun is coming up and that this is going to be a great day. There are, thankfully, few people around that early, and those who are arouse my suspicion. What the hell are they doing at six in the morning? Hmm, maybe they are going down to the ocean to fish. Then envy strikes.

Another time when I can relax is when I am doing something physical, like working in the yard, on a task that does not require any great mental concentration. It gives my mind a chance to reflect at length on various problems. I can get a perspective that is difficult to acquire sitting at a desk. Every day, a person should build in a little time for personal solitude. Even if it means pacing up and down in a room like a monk or priest, it is thinking. It rehabilitates your soul.

There has to be something in between the periods of being overprogrammed. No matter how difficult it is to find the time, the successful executive has to find some solitude. You can't just go from working hard into drinking hard or eating hard, then burning out and sleeping and then getting up, jumping in the shower, and going to work. It won't work that way. You have to have that rehabilitative time in between. If you don't do it, what is happening is that you are never truly thinking. You are never turning your mind loose and letting it sort of automatically zoom in on significant problems. It is amazing the solutions that will come to you when you are not burdened or overprogrammed and pressed; when your mind has an opportunity to work freely on its own.

A mind totally dominated by a routine that doesn't leave any time for thinking isn't capable of clear thought, innovative thought, or independent thought. That kind of mind doesn't have very much give. It can't cope with too many new situations. It cannot face new challenges, and it cannot grasp new ideas. It can't do any of these things because it won't allow itself to relax for a short time each day to look inside itself. Every leader must provide for this kind of solitude or he will surely sink.

PERSONAL STAFF

The term *personal staff* here does not refer to immediate subordinates. Those are the assistant and deputy chiefs who have line supervision over various responsibilities within the agency. *Personal staff* refers to the members of the staff of the chief executive: the people who help him process the paper work; the people who perform the inspection and control function, which incidentally should be a part of his office; and the people who do any liaison work, whether it is community relations, administrative, judicial, or legislative.

Let me give you an example. The personal staff of the president of the United States is the White House staff, as contrasted with subordinates like the secretary of state or the secretary of defense. It is extremely important never to allow the staff, or any one member of the staff, to be a dominant element around the chief executive. A good example was Haldeman in the Nixon White House. Everyone had to go through him, and all paths led through Haldeman to the president. Congressmen, other members of the White House staff, friends, anyone other than a few key cabinet officers who normally reported directly to the president, were at the mercy of one man, Haldeman. Such a person on a staff accrues power to himself, and he becomes a cynosure—the power figure as well as the power broker. He can cut off information from the boss—perhaps not maliciously, but to protect the boss—and he can make bad decisions.

Because such a person is a power figure, no one is going to want to get in trouble with him by going around him and complaining to the boss that he is, in effect, improperly obstructing the chain of command. There is no way of complaining to the president. So there is no way the boss can find out if the man who has gathered a great deal of power to himself and has been given a great deal of power by his boss is doing a bad job. And if he is doing a bad job, there is a great probability that the office of the chief executive will be doing a bad job.

Knowing this long before Watergate, I organized my personal staff so that no one person had control over me or my work. Although I have many different staff members, no one of them is *always* personally with me, and no one has to go through them to get to me. I do have a chief of staff, a deputy chief, and he hires and transfers most of my staff members with my concurrence. He does a great many things for me, but he is never sitting in my office during discussions with another assistant chief or with other members of my personal staff. People do not have to go through him to get to me. To get in to see me, people go through my secretary or my executive officer. What this does is give limited authority to many different staff members for many different things, and no single member knows what my day is like. My secretary, for example, comes in for dictation in the morning. She knows who I am writing to, but no one else sees the letters but me. She does not go to the chief of staff to get them approved. She had better not. She has instructions not to do that.

My executive officer sees me each day with all the mail that has arrived since the day before, from the police commission, from the outside world, and from managers within the department. We work together for about 45 minutes to an hour each day. Then, depending upon my schedule, there may be one of the assistant chiefs in to see me. When he is in there talking to me, nobody else is there. My immediate subordinates, the three assistant chiefs, do not need an appointment to see me; everyone else does. A captain, who processes all my paper work to the police commission may have an appointment. So, throughout the day, there is no more than one person who even knows where I have gone if I leave Parker Center. And no one can say, "Come and do business with me, because I can get things done through Ed Davis."

A personal staff should exist to make it possible for the chief executive to function at optimum effectiveness. A personal staff, in effect, is power steering, power brakes, power windows, and an automatic transmission. With the slightest touch, the chief executive can move the organization. I am always impressed by the rapidity with which things can be accomplished with the proper use of the staff. You can really get things moving. That reflects the high caliber of personnel and the limited knowledge that each subordinate has of the problems. If two or three people knew everything about my office, they might feel overwhelmed or concerned about all my problems and then fail to get the things that I need from them. When each man has his own specialty in the office, he does not have to worry about some other problem. All he should be concerned about is his area of responsibility and how he can help the chief executive from that one area.

DAILY THROUGHPUT

Regardless of what level of boss you are, lieutenant, chief, or middle manager, it is extremely important that you get today's work done today. There should be no in-baskets where things can gather. There should be no drawers where things are "kept." If it would not cost the City of Los Angeles so much money, I would have carpenters come in with saws and cut all the drawers out of all my executives' desks. I would get rid of them because I can guarantee you that their sole purpose is to hide work—at least, psychologically. The decisions that should be made and the decisions that are never going to be made are in those drawers. And there must be "daily throughput."

There is no time to constantly study things in an active organization. There is a time when things are ready and something must be done. Plans for a new building, for example, are either ready to go forward when the boss sees them or they should be sent back because they are not ready yet. Taking the specifications home in a briefcase or hiding them in a drawer is not going to do anything but make them smell. The plans are going to be totally out of date when they are finally permitted to proceed.

The importance of meeting every problem today with decisiveness cannot be stressed enough. When it is decided that either the plan goes back for more work or it goes forward for approval, the executive relieves his mind of the obsessive worry about that one particular thing. There is simply no substitute for total daily throughput. If you feel uncomfortable about a project because you do not know everything about it, just realize that you probably know everything there is to know about it at that point. Waiting a month or six weeks is not going to provide more knowledge. If you do not have the confidence to make a decision on it, then send it back for more information. There should be no in-baskets. Get rid of them. Get a sledgehammer and smash them, or burn them in a bonfire. "Pending" boxes are worse. Given enough time and a gutless manager and the whole world, every project ever invented will end up pending.

One of the critical things in managing daily throughput is, I repeat, the importance of establishing due dates, "due *within* dates." Those deadlines give plenty of time to get the job done, and then all it takes is controlling those due dates. Every day you look in and ask, "Who owes me something today?" You discover that So-and-so owes such-and-such. Well, he had better get it in. If he doesn't, you have to communicate with him. You have to discipline people to get their work done. If you don't, you permit indecisiveness and holding back. Then it is your fault.

It is only the discipline that gets the work done. They say, "With this old guy, you better get it in. If you don't, it will be very embarrassing." And it works. I have rarely seen a case where a project was so tough that it received an open deadline. An open deadline will go on and on and on, and in the end you have just failed to make a decision. If you have a hunch that you better get on top of something, assign it out right away and let some assistant play with it. But give it a short due date and then you won't wind up with nothing happening. Usually, if you don't give it that short due date, you end up regretting it. You should have forced him, when you had the instinct six months before, to come in with a recommendation in six weeks or a month, and you didn't, so then it becomes your fault.

TENURE

In the vast majority of American police departments, the chief executive serves at the pleasure of the mayor or a city manager. Because of the politics involved, there is a very high turnover rate for police chiefs. Half of all the chiefs in America today have less than 3½ years stewardship. It almost coincides with the political haymaking of mayoral elections. This constant changing of police chiefs with the changing of mayors must reflect an insecurity on the part of many chiefs and a reluctance to do anything that would be considered in any way out of sympathy with what a mayor wanted.

One of the things that holds American policing back from full professionalism is the ability of American mayors to pull the strings in controlling their police departments. In England, there is no chief of police or chief constable in any city who serves at the pleasure of any mayor or any city council. Each one is under a committee, and that committee represents all the cities, towns, boroughs, and counties that are covered by that particular chief constable. There is no direct connection between the election of a mayor or councilmen and the retention of the chief constable. There is an independence in the enforcement of the law in England, a common-sense independence that is isolated and insulated from political concerns.

What is needed here to prevent reaction by politicians toward the police department is some kind of security. There has to be some kind of due process for the removal of the chief of police. The most logical approach is that he be appointed, perhaps even by a mayor, but that his removal be only for cause. It should be necessary to prove some kind of nonfeasance or misfeasance or malfeasance in office for forcible removal. That would permit the chief executive a hearing before a duly constituted administrative tribunal and the opportunity to defend himself against such charges; and it would still allow a proper control of the department. Knowledge on the part of a chief that unless he does what the politicians tell him to do, he can be fired tomorrow, is destructive to a community.

It is my belief that the position of chief executive of a police organization should have a *minimum* of at least five years of tenure. It takes that long to really get things working well. And my own estimate of a reasonable *maximum* length of service is about eight years. Some chiefs would disagree with me, because they want to stay in longer. But after eight years, which is the maximum amount of time we allow for a president of the United States, a chief executive has had the opportunity of doing all the things he can possibly do. After that period of time, he is going to be holding the organization back. I am at my eighth year, and I will get the hell out. A new man can come in, see my mistakes, and correct them. Or he can add to what I have built. It will be his duty to take charge and guide the ship.

OPENNESS AND HONESTY

To have an effective police agency, or for that matter any kind of government organization, a sense of openness and honesty is essential. It is particularly important that police departments be, in effect, an open book to society, that there be no mystery about what a police department does. If you have to be afraid people will find something out, then it is probably wrong. The police shouldn't be doing whatever it is that is so secret.

For example, in the whole area of intelligence gathering, the Los Angeles Police Department, under its police commission, adopted a set of written guidelines on the gathering of public-disorder intelligence information. Those who

195

would overtly threaten the people—bomb throwers, potential assassins, organizations designed to disrupt the public peace or commit genocide—are recorded in our files. Those records are not open, but the department openly acknowledges that it keeps such records; and even though we never let anyone see the information, we do publish the guidelines for gathering such information.

It is absolutely essential to our acceptance by the public and our being trusted by the people that we have open, honest police service in America. There should be nothing we do that can't stand the light of day. If it can't stand the light of day, we shouldn't be doing it. Years ago, when I got my first vice squad, one of the first things I did was to tell them, "Look, it's always been against the law to tap phones in California. If I catch any of you tapping phones in order to get information on vice purveyors, I will personally throw you in jail. I'll go to the district attorney and try to take you before the grand jury and send you to San Quentin. We may have a helluva vice problem here, but we are going to cope with it in lawful fashion."

Now, not everything has to be done in the public eye. Intelligence information on the syndicate, for example, would be absolutely useless if the public could get access to that information. But keeping track of syndicate members is absolutely vital and totally justifiable.

One good test of openness is to ask, "Can citizens come in and work in the department?" The Los Angeles Police Department has a Police Reserve Corps composed of citizen volunteers. After they complete the state's minimum training standards, which takes them six months, they come in and work right in the department. That assures me and these good citizens who come in to volunteer their time that the LAPD is running an open and honest department. Our reserves are airline pilots, lawyers, doctors, garbage collectors, and secretaries. Just average citizens, including many women. If there was anything bad going on in the bowels of the department, I would probably hear about it through the Reserve

Corps. The fact that we have them there tends to keep us more honest.

A police department and every policeman in it must be absolutely honest. We can't lie—to each other or to the public. There isn't anything important enough to lie about. Of course, I was raised from a little child with an absolute belief in the commandment that says you shall not bear false witness against your neighbor. Today, for public organizations to get that kind of trust, the public must be able to believe in the leaders of them. Every policeman and every police chief has to be scrupulously honest in his deeds and honest in what he says. We can't "shine people on," as they say. We have to tell it like it is; that is what people expect. They want to hear the facts and circumstances of things. The police are not, by the nature of their work, people in which the public puts tremendous trust and confidence. People are suspicious of anyone who has power, and policemen have a great deal of power. So if the police are ever going to get the kind of help they need, they must be honest and open and candidly tell the people what the situation and condition is.

An example regarding media policy probably tells it best. One day people from a new radio station in town came in and asked to go out and talk to some of our policemen. My press guys came in and said, "This Westinghouse Network wants to go out and talk to some policemen."

I said, "You know the answer to that. Let them talk to our cops. And tell them that if they can't find any, you'll go show them some. Don't select them, just show them where they can find some policemen."

So Westinghouse went around and talked to a couple of policemen, a couple of sergeants, a couple of middle brass, and a couple of top brass. Then they broadcasted an editorial on the radio that they repeated for several days. In effect, it said, "Imagine, we went in and the chief of police let us talk to just anyone we wanted to in the department. He let that person say anything and everything that he wanted to say." They said, "How shocking this is, and how refreshing it is!"

What we didn't know was that they had gone to another law enforcement agency in the county and were told they could talk only to the top man. We weren't trying to put that agency in the middle, but that organization had a closed press policy. With a policy of openness, anyone can talk to anyone who knows anything about a particular subject. It is dangerous to put people in legal jeopardy, and the potential to prejudice a case is greater, but openness and honesty in the administration of a police department is absolutely vital to promoting public confidence in the agency so that citizens will be willing to work with the police department. If it is some kind of a mysterious, austere thing, remote, up on a mountain somewhere and you have to go to some marble palace and talk to some god, then believe me, there will be no communication, and therefore no trust.

Speaking Out

In the past, many administrators considered the function of providing community information to be a specialty. Often, the entire community communications task was delegated to a special community relations unit or to a subordinate individual. The police chief was then left with the task of carrying out the administrative responsibilities of the agency. While this appears to be a logical system, it frequently isolates the leader of the agency from both the public and members of the organization, who are then required to identify the leader with an old photograph and a television image of some real or fictional character.

Granted, the police chief cannot make a one-hour weekly appearance on a major network program, but isolation is not the only available alternative. It may be a sound management principle to use specialized units or individuals for routine information, but the ultimate responsibility for establishing credibility with the public and ensuring effective communications remains with the police chief.

During the course of a study on the police chief executive,

his latitude in expressing professional opinion on public safety issues was judged extremely important. It was discovered that 98 percent of the police chiefs and 89 percent of their superiors believed that the chief law enforcement official in our communities should speak out.[2] Damn few ever do it. Each community is different, but in every one, the success of the police mission, protection and service, is dependent upon the degree of willing cooperation and voluntary observance that can be secured from the public, and the public should know the police chief's views. A police agency cannot function outside the expressed will of the people. The police agency and the community must work together toward social order and civil peace, and good communication is vital to the maintenance of this bond.

Here is how to look at it. Once a decision is made to publicly discuss an issue and the speaker voices his opinion, everything said becomes history. The speaker, more specifically the chief executive, is now open to criticism. Even for having made comments, however honest, that lacked tact, the leader can be subjected to political or administrative sanction, and the chief executive who doesn't have community support or a political base may be asked to seek other employment.

Therefore, the smart leader will consider the subject matter that will be discussed as well as the actual supportive evidence or examples cited. Before a thought or feeling is communicated, a great deal of anticipatory thought must go into the message. For instance, the chief might want to fully describe an official investigation that resulted in an arrest. However, if the details are discussed, he may infringe upon the person's right to a fair trial. The scope of the discussion must therefore be limited and the reasons for the limitation explained.

While the climate for free expression by the chief executive differs from one locale to another, some general parameters can be discussed here. Public comments ought to be

[2]*Police Chief Executive* (Washington, D.C.: LEAA, 1976).

199

designed to stimulate public interest, relieve actual or potential community tensions, dispel rumors, and build public trust and confidence. Professional opinions should generally be limited to issues related to public safety, including potential dangers, prevalent crime or traffic problems, proposed legislation, and any other issues that may affect public safety. Once the subject matter has been tentatively selected, it is important to determine the type of impression that will be conveyed to the audience. For example, the public is often more interested in what it can do than in what cannot be done.

The idea that a public official, particularly a police official, should speak out on issues affecting his community is of great importance to me. Not just because I have done it for so long, or because the public has a right to such information, but because the public is capable of doing the right thing with it. In a sense, it is a corollary to my feelings about openness and honesty, only in this instance, there are editorial rights involved.

The police chief who does not speak out on critical matters affecting the people he serves isn't earning his pay. It's as simple as that. What he says may not always be popular, and it may cost him his job; but who would want that kind of job anyway, or would want to work under such conditions? Not me!

15

Relations
with the Media

PRESS RELATIONS

It is very important that a police agency have an open media policy. If the police are going to receive public cooperation in fighting crime, they must have a good relationship with members of the press. Through them there is a great opportunity to report to the people about crime. Crime will always be a very interesting type of news item. The media are always interested in it because it sells advertising. A media policy should permit anyone in the department who has adequate knowledge of relevant information, from the lowest to the highest ranking person, to talk to the press. This keeps the chief from having to talk to them all the time.

I don't spend very much time with the press myself, unless they catch me going around a corner or down a hallway in Parker Center. However, the press can go right to the investigator in charge of the case, or to a policeman who has handled a big field incident, and if he has all the facts at his disposal, he is, by my rule, authorized to talk to the media.

Some agencies have, as previously mentioned, closed press policies, which provide that only the chief or the sheriff may communicate with the press. Well, that creates a bottle-neck through which nothing will ever pass. We have a press relations section whose sole function is to answer questions of the media. We have one Mexican-American officer who is liaison to the Spanish-speaking media. We have Spanish-language radio, television, and newspapers in Los Angeles, and they can call this Spanish-speaking officer and he can run anything down for them. We also have one black officer who services the black press, and we have three other officers who handle the rest of it. Of course, the black and Mexican officers also help with the general media information problems. We don't issue PR-type press releases from this office. There has never been a press release designed to boost some politician or executive.

Media problems are usually associated with service diffi-culties in getting the facts and running with the story. We put out very few press releases, because they are viewed by the media people as propaganda, and far too often they really are propaganda. The few we do put out are to provide a report that has been requested by media people, on a major crime or unusual event. These are responsive releases, not pronouncements.

The media generally spook out things that are interest-ing, and they ask their own questions about the subject being reported. They don't need propaganda. Sometimes media people want to conduct a special feature that may involve numerous resources. Somebody may have to sit down with them and spend a great deal of time filling reporters in on something. There may even be a need to have someone dig into files and get information for them. That is what we call "cold news." "Hot news" is information of current interest, and any media representative is entitled to get it. If they want to know anything that can legally be given, such as the name of the suspect who was arrested, we will give it to them. If they want to know any of the facts or circumstances that are appropriate to release, we will release that information too. On special-feature material, we evaluate the background of the paper and the writer, and if he is an antipolice guy who is out to hang us, we don't provide him with the information to hang us. If he has a reputation for being objective and fair, we will evaluate whether we can take the time for the feature story. Some parts of the media occasionally sound off with tirades against the department or the chief, and we cut them off in terms of feature stories. We're not going to give them the rope to hang us either. But "hot news" is available to all bona fide news-media people, and it goes to all of them at the same time, no preferential treatment.

There are three categories of cases that we do not give information out on. First and foremost is national security. For example, I had to know about our raising the Russian submarine because of the theft at Howard Hughes's offices in Los Angeles, but I wouldn't tell anyone. The *New York Times* and the local press all tried to get that information, but there was no way they were going to get it from me, because it involved the security of the American people. Eventually, some person released the information; it could have resulted in a big international blowup over our raising a Russian submarine from Pacific waters. That story should not have been released, even though some members of the media had a different view of it.

Second, if a person's right to a fair trial is apt to be imperiled by pretrial publicity, information should not be released. The British system requires the press to say nothing about a case until after the trial is over. Some day we may come to that in America, because many people in notorious cases are virtually convicted in the media before they ever get a trial. The police, however, should never contribute to a media trial. We frequently close down any information on notorious cases and advise reporters to sort out the facts in a court or through good old-fashioned research. A judge can and should protect the rights of the accused in the court, but he may have difficulty extending his power outside the court-room.

Finally, where release of the information will interfere with an ongoing investigation, we withhold the facts. For example, in a kidnapping case, if a relative of the victim was going out to some secret location to make a money drop, the media, if they could, would have cars following the relative to the drop site. This parade would, of course, scare the suspect away, the police might never catch the kidnapper, and the hostage might even be killed. In those cases, we refuse to give the media any information.

When we had to move Emily and William Harris from northern California to Los Angeles, we had the plane taxi to a remote part of the runway. We discharged these two people there and had each one of them picked up in a helicopter, after their hands were very securely fixed to the chains around their waists. Then we had the pilot land on the roof of the police building. Bill Harris went to our jail and Emily Harris was taken to the county jail for women. The press didn't even get a chance to take a picture. We were concerned about the possibility that some small group of people would attempt to rescue them. Further, there was a possibility of their getting unnecessary pretrial publicity. So we just cut the media out of the entire process.

But generally, we try to accommodate the media where we can. The general rule is to cooperate with the media on hot news—and *all* the media, whether you like them or not. They are all entitled to it because the people are entitled to the information. This open press policy is predicated on the democratic principle. For a democracy to operate effectively, you must have an informed public, and a free press is absolutely vital to an informed public. The more we can do to assist the free press in informing the populace about police work, the better off the country is going to be. It becomes our obligation to cooperate with the media. It's not just something that's nice to do; it is an obligation.

We do have some typically dumb editorials, but that's part of a free press. The press is entitled to it. Anyone can rebut editorials on radio and television, and I give speeches sometimes about the media. Once I gave a whole 40-minute lecture on the media and intellectual corruption. The press is not organized the way the police are. They are not under any potential threat of discipline, and they are probably the most undisciplined profession in America; but like wives, they are vital.

Under the First Amendment to our Constitution, freedom of the press is specifically guaranteed, and I suppose it must operate as it does. It is the only press we have, and it should be able to editorialize against me, publish cartoons against me, slant news stories against me. The public will eventually figure out what is right. We cannot legislate control over the press, because once you do that, the press is no longer free. What I pray for is the day when the media create their own sense of ethics and impose discipline upon themselves.

MEDIA APPEARANCES

Once in a while, people in the broadcast industry invite a public official to speak on a particular program strictly for the purpose of giving that official an opportunity to express himself. They may say, "We want to help you, Chief, and anything you want to say is okay." But there are not many such occasions. In most cases, what the media want to do is spark controversy. They want to have their steel hit flint, and they want sparks. Their whole method of operations is designed to generate heat and get you embroiled in a controversy. Why? Controversy sells newspapers, and it is more interesting. Besides, it is more fun.

In a way, it is a contest—the Christians versus the lions. You know: Lions, 3; Christians, 0. People down through history have enjoyed such contests. That is why they go to bullfights; that is why they go to prizefights and football games. People like contests and controversy. One thing you can bet on, if the media people are average and normal, they know they are going to sell a lot more advertising by having controversy. You can expect controversy and you should be prepared for controversy.

Personally, I enjoy it. What I try to do before I go on one of these programs is say, "If I were out to get Ed Davis, what would I attack him on today?" I think back on all the things I have done in the previous few months. I have seldom been surprised by my adversaries. In fact, in the eight years that I have been on radio and television, they have done precisely what I thought they would. What they are going to try and do is create a fight between two personalities. I think what I am going to say about a subject if I am asked. All you need is an answer. I might tell them that I am not interested in a fight, that I am just interested in keeping the other guy's hands out of my pockets. I am willing to get along with him as long as he does not steal from me. I might not quite say it that way on television, but I will get that impression across, because the media is for sure going to ask personality questions.

They have asked me if I was anticipating running for mayor. Of course, the answer is yes. I tell them that I am already in my eighth term as mayor of Chatsworth, and I am going to run for my ninth term next year. It is an honorary position, an appointment by the chamber of commerce. I do not want to be the mayor of a big city; but they do not want to hear me say, "No."

As crazy as the questions are, they can be anticipated. All the motivation they attribute to you will be evil, self-serving, and egotistical. You can count on it. You must, therefore, look back over the past several months and think about the subject matter and the probable angles of attack and how you can respond to the attack. The media have great morgue files and they can gather information from numerous sources. Their intelligence capability is certainly better than that of the police, and may even be better than the capability of the federal government. So, like a Boy Scout, you must be prepared!

PUBLIC APPEARANCES

The chief executive is paid to run his organization, and that takes a great deal of internal time for proper administration. It does not leave very much time for sitting around being a decoration at a luncheon business meeting or an evening banquet table. Any time spent at a meeting should be spent communicating with people as a participant or principal speaker. The whole purpose of the use of this time is to communicate and discuss problems with people and to solicit from people their cooperation. That won't be accomplished by sitting as an ornament at the head table.

Ornamentation is a terribly wasteful expenditure of time; it is very hard on the digestive tract, and it broadens the rear end. Further, it does not really contribute much of anything. It is very hard work for a chief executive to see that the time he spend in attempting to communicate to the public is done with the greatest amount of leverage. It can be maximized through such methods of communication as radio and television. A few minutes there will do more than months of going around personally meeting people at private organizational functions.

So you must make a very firm policy of not being an ornament at any head table. You want to be there only when you are asked to speak and are allowed to communicate your views to the group assembled. And you do the very minimum amount of that. I make almost no luncheon appearances, because they steal time out of the prime part of my day. Can speeches be avoided? Not by a long shot. But they can be productive.

Notwithstanding those objections, speaking is generally fun. Evening speeches do take energy and may rob you of some vigor the next day, but they keep you in touch. There are some groups that simply have to see you in person. The whole purpose of any public appearance should be advancing the objectives of the organization.

One method of giving speeches that I like to use frequently is to tell the people that I have only a little bit to say and it will take about five minutes to tell—perhaps about some new development or event. Then people tell me what they would like to have me talk about, and I write down those subjects on a piece of paper. Pretty soon there are eight or ten subjects that become my speech.

The advantage of this technique is that you have learned what is on the minds of your audience. It may surprise you to learn that their concerns are not what you perceived them to be. They might not be concerned about what you think they should be concerned about. If you are going to be responsive to the needs of the people, you have to get some feedback from them. Now, keep those slips of paper over the years, and you can look back over them and see that a year ago they were interested in such-and-such, but no one is concerned with that problem any more. You might throw the paper away. The audience may not be right in what they think the problems are, but they are the people and their fears are realities to them, so it is extremely important that the executive listen.

Most important, a government executive should look to the valuable resources of radio and television to communicate the problems and the need for cooperation to the public. You can accomplish a great deal in a 30-minute question-and-answer session with three reporters. I can tell from my mail after one of these appearances that this has much more impact than giving a hundred speeches at night to a hundred different groups.

16

Organizational Policy

Every organization is a living, breathing, active product of society. Yet far too many organizations, especially in government, have lost their vitality, principally because of a loss of self-generation by subordinate supportive units. An organization must be self-actuating at its most basic unit level, and the chief executive should set forth the objectives, policies, and principles of the organization in as explicit a form as possible. If people in the organization understand these objectives, policies, and principles, they can effectively do their work without bothering their bosses.

Now, there was a time in the LAPD when policy was something that existed only in the mind of the chief executive. I specifically recall a mission that I was given by Bill Parker, my chief, when I was a young lieutenant. He said, "Lieutenant, you are going to write the manual of the Los Angeles Police Department."

I said, "I just got through writing training bulletins, and I am tired of doing staff work. I want to return to the field."

He repeated, clearly and as though I had some difficulty hearing, "Lieutenant, you are going to write the manual of the Los Angeles Police Department."

Then I understood what he was saying. I replied, "Yes, sir."

He told me to come back and tell him what would be needed for the job. I left, made my plan to write the manual, and returned to him a short time later. I said, "I'll need 1,000 square feet of office space, ten people, X number of typewriters, and X amount of paper. We plan to write the manual in this manner: Volume I will be the policies and objectives of the Los Angeles Police Department; Volume II will be the organization of the Los Angeles Police Department; Volume III will be the management rules of the Los Angeles Police Department; Volume IV will be the field procedures of the department; and Volume V will cover clerical matters."

He said, "Fine, go ahead and get to work." We got four volumes completed, but when we tried to pin him down on policy, he refused to be pinned down. He would not put policy in writing, except for a vague statement on community relations.

The first four volumes were completed in 1952. Seventeen years later, as chief of police, I was able to start putting some sections into the policy volume. We now have our 20 principles there, and many other things.

One thing I have always known was that decisions considered to be out of policy would be criticized by the department. Well, if that was the case, then people should be told what the policy was. A doctrine must be set forth. A church sets forth a doctrine so that a priest or minister does not have to run to the bishop or the head of the church to find out what should or should not be done. The policy must be clear and also broad enough to permit organizational growth and initiative. When I became chief, I was determined to give my department a doctrine, so that my people would have something to follow besides the verbal opinion of their boss, whoever he or she might be.

A SYSTEM OF BELIEFS

People generally do what they do based upon a system of beliefs. Most of us acquire these beliefs out of experience. We get them from our early training at home. We get them from our religion. This applies to all professions, including mine.

It is truly important that we try to generate in police officers, as well as our other employees, a system of beliefs or principles to guide them. Such a system should automatically guide a police officer's behavior on the job, behavior that must be consistent with the beliefs of the organization. Because of the nature of police work and the nature of the things the police deal with, which are generally negative, police officers frequently develop a pretty sour belief system. Organizational guidelines and policies are meant to diminish that sourness. Any belief system needs help from good managers and supervisors to bring about a conversion or reinforcement of those principles.

Philosophy vs. Action

Before there can be action, there must be a concept, some kind of belief. Probably one of the greatest things a leader can leave behind him, whether he is a supervisor or a manager, or even the chief executive, is not what he has specifically accomplished, but rather a philosophy—a philosophy that people can believe in. In policing, most of the philosophies, as mentioned earlier, were cultivated during seven years of debate in Parliament by Sir Robert Peel and formulated in 1829. The creation of this philosophy was far more important than the development of the Metropolitan Police Department, or Scotland Yard.

Abraham Lincoln was in many ways a failure most of his life. Yet Lincoln left us an important philosophy about governing and about perseverance in the face of adversity. It could be said that Jesus Christ was a failure, in terms of material success in this world. He never had a church of his own; he just stood out there on the sand and preached. He didn't own a house, or a cart, or much of anything else. But that young man, who died when he was 33, left a philosophy behind him that has been talked about all over the world for 2,000 years. Because of his thinking, and particularly the philosophy he talked about, he left something that has made the world a much better place in which to live. Even non-Christians agree that Jesus was a great man—not necessarily for what he did, but for what he believed in and the philosophy that he left.

So a police sergeant, lieutenant, or captain doesn't have to win to be successful. He might plant a seed if he believes in the right things and tries to lead in the right way. It is these planted seeds that potentially bear the fruit of a new philosophy and multiply success. An idea passed on may make for a better department or a safer community because of what that leader believed in. He must believe in something and live by it first before he can get something out of it. Perhaps—and this happens—he won't get anything out of it, but those who follow will. The future result is far more important than any personal success.

PRINCIPLES—A CREED

There must be a creed, a set of beliefs, and a set of objectives for an organization. These must be written out so that every member of the organization can look to them as objectives of the agency. There must be set forth, for example, the belief that the police must work with the people; the belief that the brass must work with policemen; the belief that the police must work with one another; and the belief that the police must work with the criminal justice system. All these beliefs should be incorporated into the agency's fundamental philosophy in the form of a creed.

A creed should be written out so that it can be inculcated into new people who come to the organization and can penetrate the minds of the older ones who may have joined the department when the creed was not explicitly stated. Frankly, I worked as a policeman for a long time trying to figure out what the hell my superiors wanted me to do. I knew one thing: So many tickets a day would keep the sergeant away. But it was hard for me to be like some of the people who wrote large numbers of tickets. One man who worked with me when I was a young policeman was an absolute idiot, but the sergeants thought he was great because he wrote more tickets than anyone else. You knew that you had to get so many felony arrests and you had to get so many misdemeanor arrests and you had to write so many field interview cards. That was the only thing I was ever able to figure out in terms of any policy set forth by the chief of police or the police commission.

You knew that if you did something wrong, or something that they considered wrong, you would receive some type of discipline. Yet you never really knew what it was that they considered wrong. Of course, I did know, for instance, that you should not drink on duty; but I did not know what the department's overall objectives were. Without a full set of objectives, there will be no principles that can be believed in. Every policeman needs a statement that he can read. Those principles must be understandable, so that every member of the organization can appreciate them and get moving in the same direction. Those principles will go a long way in cutting down on the need for guessing.

We have 20 principles on the Los Angeles Police Department. They are set forth in Chapter 17. If you are a member of my department, you believe in them. It is like a religious faith: You believe in the territorial imperative and put it to use; you believe that people working together can help to reduce crime. Those are some of the beliefs. They are simple enough. Yes, there are some older, recalcitrant members who do not believe in anything, who do not want to believe in the principles, but there are many young ones who want to believe. The old chief goes around and checks on them now and then, rewarding the ones who know the principles and not rewarding the ones who choose not to know them. I have many specific assignment options with staff and command officers, and I reward the hard-working people who care about the principles of the organization. The believers get ahead on my department. They do not have to come and say, "Dad, what shall we believe in?" They have the catechism: the 20 management principles of the Los Angeles Police Department. I have even threatened to make a set of rosary beads out of these principles for those who do not understand them, so if they forget them, all they have to do is take them out and begin chanting.

During my earlier years on the department, I represented my fellow officers as a lieutenant and as a captain, and I knew that there existed a lack of understanding of what management wanted in terms of functional objectives. There was no way to figure out what those top managers downtown wanted. As a captain I would see to it that crime was crushed, and I would figure that this effort would be appreciated. Someone might even pat me on the back. Instead, they sent an inspector down and he said, "Davis, we have an eye on you. We are watching and we know that you are doing something funny here. You had better be careful."

I thought to myself, "Why, you S.O.B.'s when I clean up an area and make it safe for human beings by running out all the bad guys, you come down and tell me that you and the chief have got an eye on me. Instead of saying that

I am doing a good job, you tell me that I have to be careful."

I may have used methods that would not be totally satisfactory to today's Supreme Court, but they were okay then and they were effective. They got the job done. I did not let my men beat people up or treat them unreasonably, but I didn't always wait until a criminal act was completed to move in. Most policemen know who the rotten parasites are, and they generally do not need some judge to tell them what is good for the community. However, the comments of this inspector just overwhelmed me. His comments and his tone were discouraging to me. I had thought I was getting support from downtown.

I was a member of the board of directors for the Los Angeles Police Protective League, our employee organization, which was involved in getting better wages and other benefits for members. I had been assigned to records, which was a pretty dull place to be. Then when a big vice scandal broke, they sent me to the involved division and they told me they were watching me.

As soon as my methods proved successful in my division, the area inspector called an area meeting. (An area then was composed of several similar divisions with similar problems.) At the meeting, the inspector was seated at the head of the table in this rather large room. He said, "In Area Two we have a serious vice problem, and I think we ought to start working the whores this way. We might also start working the bookmakers this way." He failed to indicate that I had used these methods in my division and that they had worked. He never said, "Davis invented this thing and I want to give him credit." He just established the new method as his policy.

Here I had had my neck out, trying to accomplish the objectives set forth. If my methods had not worked, it was my head; the brass was going to discipline me, not the area inspector. Yet, when I had resolved most of the problems of the division, and my methods were taken by this inspector and standardized, no one thanked me or told me that I was doing a good job. All along, I never really knew what they wanted. I became convinced that management had a responsibility to tell people what was expected of them.

If management has indicated what it wants and the subordinate has carried out the intent of the instructions and utilized some of his own initiative and judgment, then the employee should be told that management approves. If he is lucky, the employee might even be commended. But if he is not provided with some knowledge of what management expects, then management makes it extremely difficult, if not impossible, for the employee to function. This problem can be easily resolved by giving people a statement of principles, a document that tells them what is expected and how the organization thinks in any given area.

17

The Management
Principles of
the Los Angeles
Police Department

Here are the *Management Principles of the Los Angeles Police Department*. These principles form the basis of policy and guide the organization's effort:

Principle I: Reverence for the Law: The main thrust of a peace officer's duties consists of an attempt to enforce the law. In our application of the law we must do it within the legal spirit so clearly set forth by the framers of the Bill of Rights which was an original part of our Constitution. That bill has as its purpose elevating the rights of each citizen to a position co-equal with the state which might accuse him. Its purpose is to provide for an enforcement of the law with fundamental fairness and equity. Because of the Bill of Rights, the dignity of the individual person in America was placed in an almost sacred position of importance.

A peace officer's enforcement should not be done in grudging adherence to the legal rights of the accused, but in sincere spirit of seeing that every accused person is given all of his rights as far as it is within the powers of the police.

In the discharge of our enforcement of criminal statutes, the peace officer must scrupulously avoid any conduct which would make him a violator of the law. The solution of a crime, or the arrest of a lawbreaker, can never justify the peace officer's committing a felony as an expedient for the enforcement of the law.

We peace officers should do our utmost to foster a reverence for the law. We can start best by displaying a reverence for the legal rights of our fellow citizens and a reverence for the law itself.

Principle II: Crime Prevention Top Priority: The basic mission for which the police exist is to prevent crime and disorder as an alternative to repression by military force and severity of legal punishment. When the police fail to prevent crime, it becomes important to apprehend the person responsible for the crime and gather all evidence that might be used in a subsequent trial.

Principle III: Public Approbation of Police: The ability of the police to perform their duties is dependent upon public approval of police existence, actions, behavior, and the ability of the police to secure and maintain public respect.

Principle IV: Voluntary Law Observance: The police must secure the willing cooperation of the public in voluntary observance of the law in order to be able to secure and maintain the respect and approval of the public.

Principle V: Public Cooperation: The degree of public cooperation that can be secured diminishes, proportionately, the necessity for the use of physical force and compulsion in achieving police objectives.

Principle VI: Impartial Friendly Enforcement: The police seek and preserve public favor, not by catering to public opinion, but by constantly demonstrating absolutely impartial service to the law without regard to the justice or injustice of the substance of individual laws; by readily offering individual service and friendship to all members of society without regard to their race or social standing; by the ready exercise of courtesy and friendly good humor; and by readily offering individual sacrifice in protecting and preserving life.

Principle VII: Minimum Use of Force: The police should use physical force to the extent necessary to secure observance of the law or to restore order only when the exercise of persuasion, advice, and warning is found to be insufficient to achieve police objectives; and police should use only the reasonable amount of physical force which is necessary on any particular occasion for achieving a police objective.

Principle VIII: Public Is the Police: The police at all times should maintain a relationship with the public that gives reality to the historic tradition that the police are the public and that the public is the police; the police are the only members of the public who are paid to give full-time attention to duties which are incumbent on every citizen in the interest of community welfare.

Principle IX: Limit of Police Power: The police should always direct their actions strictly toward their functions and never appear to usurp the powers of the judiciary by avenging individuals or the state, or authoritatively judging guilt or punishing the guilty.

Principle X: Test of Police Effectiveness: The test of police effectiveness is the absence of crime and the presence of public order. It is not the evidence of police action in dealing with crime and disorder.

Principle XI: People Working with Police: The task of crime prevention cannot be accomplished by the police alone.

This task necessarily requires the willing cooperation of both the police and the public, working together toward a common goal.

Principle XII: People Working with People: Since the police cannot be expected to be on every residential or business block every hour of the day, a process must be developed whereby each person becomes concerned with the welfare and safety of his neighborhood. When people are working with other people in their neighborhood, they can effectiveiy reduce crime.

Principle XIII: Managers Working with Police: Only line police officers perform the tasks for which police were created. They are the operating professionals. Supervisors and managers exist to define problems, to establish objectives, and to assist line police officers in the accomplishment of the police mission.

The evaluation of a manager should be based on the improvement and excellence of his subordinates in the achievement of organizational goals. The life blood of good management is thoroughly systematic, two-way circulation of information, feelings, and perceptions throughout the organization.

Principle XIV: Police Working with Police: For many reasons, some specialization of work is necessary. Specialization should be created only when vitally necessary. When specialization is created, organization should be adjusted to ensure that the specialists and generalists who serve the same citizens work closely together on the common problems in as informal an organizational structure as possible. This will tend to ensure a unity of effort, resources, and the effective service to a common goal.

Principle XV: Police Working with Criminal Justice System: It must be recognized that the police and the people alone cannot successfully resolve the problems of crime. The criminal justice system as a whole, in order to properly serve the public, must operate as a total system with all of its various elements working together. The close cooperation of the police with prosecutors, courts, and correctional officers is necessary in order to ensure the development of a safer community.

Principle XVI: Police/Press Relationships: One of the first and most fundamental considerations of this nation's founders in drafting the Bill of Rights was to provide for a free press as an essential element of the First Amendment to the Constitution. They recognized that a well-informed citizenry is vital to the effective functioning of a democracy. Police operations profoundly affect the public and therefore arouse substantial public interest. Likewise, public interest and public cooperation bear significantly on the successful accomplishment of any police mission. The police should make every reasonable effort to serve the needs of the media in informing the public about crime and other police problems. This should be done with an attitude of openness and frankness whenever possible. The media should have access at the lowest level in a department, to personnel who are fully informed about the subject of a press inquiry. The media should be told all that can be told that will not impinge on a person's right to a fair trial, seriously impede a criminal investigation, imperil a human life, or seriously endanger the security of the people. In such cases, the minimum information should be given which will not impinge on the four areas and we should merely state that nothing more can be said.

In all other matters in our relationship with the media dealing with current news, every member of the department should make every reasonable effort consistent with accomplishing the police task in providing the media representatives with full and accurate material.

Principle XVII: Management by Objectives: In order to effectively deal with the most important problems, objectives must be established. The establishment of objectives and the means used to ensure that they are reached must include the participation of those involved in the task. The setting of an objective has very little meaning without the participation of those involved.

Principle XVIII: Management by Participation: Since employees are greatly influenced by decisions that are made and objectives that are established, it is important for them to be able to provide input into the methods utilized to reach these decisions. Employees should be encouraged to make recommendations which might lead to an improvement in the delivery of police services and assist in the furtherance of the department's meeting its objective.

Principle XIX: Territorial Imperative: Police work is one of the most personal of all personal services. It deals with human beings in life-and-death situations. The police officers and the people they serve must be as close as possible, and where possible must know one another. Such closeness can generate the police–citizen cooperation necessary for the involvement of the whole community in community protection. Organization of assignments should ensure that the same police and the same citizens have an opportunity to continuously work for the protection of a specific community. Strength through interacting together and working together on common problems can be enhanced through officers and the people feeling at home with one another in an atmosphere of mutual cooperation. This may be described as a utilization of the "territorial imperative."

Principle XX: Openness and Honesty: For police-public cooperation, there must be respect of the police by the public. This is best ensured by optimum openness of the department in its operations. A general feeling and reality of openness must pervade the police organization. Above all, the police officer must be consistently open, honest, and trustful in all matters. A combination of honesty and openness will effectively develop respect in the community for the police and make it possible for citizens to come to them with problems and information. Where this trust does not exist because of a lack of honesty or openness, the channels of communication between the police and the public are clogged and the police must desperately struggle on alone.

18

The Five Frontiers
of Police Work

Since the mid-1960s, a new era has begun for the law enforcement community in America. Born of the tragic urban riots of that era, some of the proposals to reshape the police role in our society were admittedly revolutionary. In many instances, a whole reworking of our governmental process would have been required to satisfy some elements demanding change. After a period of defensiveness, the police have come to recognize a need for openness with the communities they serve.

Our premise today is that we do have urban problems, mainly the crime problem, and that we must define that problem better if we are going to solve it. Defining that problem means looking at every dimension and facet of it. Once it has been thoroughly defined, the solution isn't really that difficult.

THE FRONTIERS

Once the specific problem is defined, we must seek to put into motion several interactions. We have to get the *people and the police working together;* the *people and the people working together;* the *police, the true line professionals, working with their superiors;* the *police officers working with other officers;* and the *police working with the rest of the criminal justice system.* None of these things have really been done well in America. In some other countries, this system is actually a part of the culture.

People and Police

In 1970, the Basic-Car Plan was implemented in Los Angeles on a citywide basis. It was, as mentioned earlier, an attempt to tie the policemen down to a certain geographical area of responsibility; in other words, an attempt to structure the concept of the "territorial imperative." Out of it we hoped would come a new relationship between the policeman and the people he was serving.

That concept has been expanded to team policing. We now have meetings with neighbors in private residences, discussing local problems, rather than large, community-type meetings where individual concerns are often lost. The police are the catalytic agent for the adoption of many neighborhood programs. They advise on and discuss various local problems, but the real effectiveness of such meetings depends, to a very large extent, upon the concern and commitment of neighbors to one another. The police are not the key to crime prevention. That is a responsibility of the community.

People and People

The idea of people working with other people is well illustrated by our local antiburglar campaign, "Neighborhood Watch." The need seems obvious. It certainly involves more than just burglary, because it means that people are their neighbors' keepers in many ways. As a result, we have observed the development of friendly associations between people who might never have spoken to one another before.

In addition to helping citizens help themselves against the encroachment of crime, Neighborhood Watch has also generated a new social atmosphere, a social organization within communities, which was generally lacking in most metropolitan areas. It embraces one of the factors that we have known must be accomplished before crime could be successfully abated. After all, the roots of our democratic republic and of our system of policing were founded upon the notion of peoples working together toward a common objective, be it freedom or security.

Police and Superiors

In Los Angeles, we have moved the deputy chiefs out of their swivel chairs in police headquarters into the field where the action is, so that when they come to make decisions, they can have a real feel for what is needed and what the attitudes of people are. They are no longer working with abstract pieces of paper. They are working with people. We have changed from a functional organizational structure, where we had the mythical chief of detectives and chief of patrol, to a decentralized operation where the chiefs have responsibility for a specific piece of turf. By putting the chiefs in charge of an area and physically placing them in that area, we have them more attuned to the policing problems. Further, they have a more significant personal feeling about their jobs.

One chief expressed it by saying, "When I was in charge of patrol, I was an administrator in the worst sense of the word. I was dealing with little pieces of paper. Now, under decentralization, I am dealing with people and their problems. I really feel as though I can get something done." That is what it means to have police officers working with their superiors. They know that someone is there. They know that someone cares, someone who can get things done.

Police and Police

Team policing is perhaps the best example of what real organizational teamwork means. Patrol officers and investigators work together on specific area problems. They share a sense of responsibility for the same piece of turf. Each member of that team relies upon other members to reduce crime and secure peace for the people of that community. The uniformed men and the investigators define problems together, and they develop some solutions.

It also means a real type of participative management. Some specialization might be necessary—homicide investigations, for example—but the concept of team policing means that the people actually performing the function will perceive themselves as being at one against the problem of crime. They openly discuss mutual problems and develop strategies.

Police and the Criminal Justice System

The last frontier that must be confronted, although it is by no means the least important, is bringing the police together with the criminal justice system. There has never been a real attempt to bring together the principals involved in the administration of justice in order to properly serve the people. Approximately five years ago, I set up an organization that is sometimes described as the Los Angeles County Criminal Justice Group. It is composed of the county sheriff, the district attorney, the city attorney, the public defender, the presiding judges of the superior and municipal courts, the president of the local bar association, the chief probation officer, and the state's chief of corrections. We sit down together each month and discuss our common problems. This is a serious attempt to get the system to operate at its maximum to better serve the people.

A demonstration of the effectiveness of the criminal justice group occurred as the result of a problem involving serious gang violence. To combat it, the group organized an ad hoc committee on juvenile justice. All the principals brought sufficient pressure on the system to create some very positive results. The juvenile court was expanded to ensure that justice would be swift, prosecutors were assigned to each court, and in one area of the city we began to experiment with a community-type juvenile justice center. It really helped.

We could cut crime in half in this country without too much effort it we could get the whole criminal justice system together and concerned. It takes a resolved commitment to cut crime.

Those five frontiers can spell success for our cities and for the people we serve. They can mean less crime and a more peaceful existence for our communities. By approaching all five frontiers boldly, it is my belief, we can do something positive about crime. In my city, we have come a long way toward doing just that.

SHARING THE PRINCIPLES
WITH THE COMMUNITY

Not only must an organization have a creed, written policies and principles, so that all employees can understand them; and not only must we cross the five frontiers to bring about the objectives embodied in those principles, if there is going to be a partnership between the organization and the public, there must be a sharing with the public of those organizational beliefs, policies, and objectives. If partners are going to work effectively together, they must be able to understand what the company is in business for.

Communication with the public cannot be achieved in any single fashion. Certainly, things can be written out and given to people who want them. Written material can also be given to the media. Obviously, there has to be a constant flow of communication to the public from all levels of the organization, from the head of agency down to the operational level within any particular area. If there is no programmed communication at every level, some of the employees can become isolated from society and its problems, and society will also become isolated from the organization.

So a chief executive and the top brass must look at what their obligations are in this communication process. They must structure the use of their time for external communication to various segments of the community, such as the chamber of commerce, businessmen's groups, and service clubs, as well as some of the leadership in various ethnic and religious organizations in society. There are, for example, police/clergy councils, a very special group in my community, which have become a part of our organization. If they were not structured into the organization, there would be no communication.

The best way to communicate your policies to the community is through those people who have a tremendous impact on the behavior of other people, such as teachers, religious leaders, and people in the electronic media—not just in the news field, but in general programming and production. They can be called the "multipliers of influence." If you are going to get the joint message out to them on how to cut crime, for example, it is only going to happen if you select the people to meet and find out how best to go about meeting with them. That means more than just responding to people who want you to come and talk to them. It requires a seeking out of those people who should be brought in or who should be met with. It is a difficult process, because the most powerful, the ones with the greatest voice to the people, the ones with the greatest impact, do not have to come in and see you.

There was a Baptist preacher in my own community who had built the biggest congregation west of the Mississippi River. He had just thousands and thousands of families joining the First Baptist Church. The Reverend Fickett did not have to come to me; but I made sure that he and I got together on many important issues, things that were important to the police department. The assistance that was gained from his church was decisive in helping my department in its efforts to have the death penalty restored in California. His church had a very large part in many other successes in our city.

Now, the people who are going to come to you frequently, the ones who make great demands on your time, are usually very good-hearted and just want to help. But sometimes they are people who want to build themselves in the process; it is important to be careful and know the difference. There are many important people who will never solicit communication and must be sought out. They have enough to do that they really do not need you. At least, they do not realize that they need you. You have to structure that communication to them.

In Los Angeles, we have communication directly to the public from the chief down through the various levels, but too frequently, middle management gets away with virtually no fixed communication responsibility. When I cannot fulfill a request personally, I assign people who would otherwise be going home at five o'clock. My assistant and deputy chiefs are told, "You are going to go out and give a speech tonight, because I have to attend another gathering."

In my department, for more than six years now, personnel right down to the level of policeman have been given a fixed responsibility for setting up meetings with the public in various parts of their beat, particularly the areas with the greatest need. Most frequently, those meetings are where people have the greatest fear of crime or where we know crime seems to be heading, and we want to get there first and galvanize those citizens into meeting it head on, together. It has been a very effective method of communicating the police department's business, telling them what our partnership is all about.

The partnership is really quite one-sided. There are only two of us to each thousand citizens. It is pretty obvious that we are not going to overwhelm them by getting to everyone. But if we just sat back, we would never get our message across. The public must be taught that it can't be saved by a police department, but that, working together with the police department, it can make the community much safer. This involves working in an active partnership, and I mean really working, actually doing things physically that take effort and energy.

If we could intensify the work we do with the people, five years later we could undoubtedly have only half the crime we had before. Here we live with a constantly increasing rate of serious crime, crime that makes people fearful of others. We have lovely communities with good, open people, and gradually a few bad guys in their midst start doing such reprehensible things that people become afraid of one another.

It is possible that smaller communities have more to lose than any of the major cities, where the fear of crime has been the hallmark for several decades. But even 20 years ago, people in the very large cities worked together; today, we can see what happens to a city when the fear of crime permeates it and takes root. The financial troubles of some of the big cities are part of that same mess. The garbagemen and the firemen and the cops can hold people up for more demands because of their terrible fears. Remember the police strikes of the last several years. Even the policemen can become terrorists, just as the garbagemen can.

It is sad that crime is such a big thing and that is makes us worry about policemen causing more problems through unreasonable strikes. Unfortunately, crime *is* that big. It creates a great deal of fear. Any community can become like some major cities, where people snarl at one another, where people are afraid of one another, where tourists are not inclined to go out onto the street because the word is out that the city is unsafe. People have to go to some major cities for business reasons, because that is where a large number of corporate offices have remained, but business is the only thing that keeps them going there. Some big cities are not "fun cities" any more.

Communication with the public is absolutely vital. When communication ceases, people become totally isolated from one another and the whole community suffers. At some point, the police no longer love the people they serve, even though they came from among those people and their roots may still be there. With communication, those roots need not wither and that love can be restored.

ORGANIZED CITIZEN INVOLVEMENT

To make something that we believe work effectively, we frequently have to institutionalize it. Unfortunately, sometimes the institution lasts beyond the point where it effectively and efficiently provides a designed service. Public institutions, in particular, tend to exist in perpetuity.

Citizens' groups, on the other hand, generally evolve informally, and that is good. My department has tried to gain the benefit of this grass-roots concept as much as possible. We have numerous citizens' programs that we have tried to institutionalize. For example, we have an Explorer Scout program for teen-aged boys and girls. For the Explorer program to be significant, the Explorers must engage in some phases of police work and some phases of police/community work. During the Manson murder case, they went out and searched hillsides for evidence. Police manpower is a pretty scarce commodity, and there are many activities in which

Explorers can properly reduce the amount of police man-power necessary.

In my view, the best use of Explorers has been with crime-deterrence programs, through our Junior Neighborhood Watch, where Explorers instead of policemen set up meetings with younger neighborhood kids. Kids from 9 to 12 years old meet for the purpose of having a Junior Neighborhood Watch group. They have been extremely effective in taking care of their neighborhoods, and it has not cost the taxpayers one cent. The Explorer program gives these young ladies and gentlemen a significant role to play. If the objective of the police service is to reduce crime, and if someone exploring law enforcement as a career can exercise the process of leader-ship while he is rather young and able to see objectively that his efforts significantly reduce crime, then you have the makings of a good police officer. Of course, one of the secret motivations behind the Explorer program is to induce these kids to become police officers.

Another official volunteer organization we have found to be successful is our Police Reserve Corps. We provide our reserves with all the training required by state law for a police officer—more than 300 hours of basic police training, including shooting, self-defense, the law, search and seizure, and other specialized courses. Then, after graduation, they are full peace officers.

Police Reserves can be one of the greatest programs of a police agency. At no real expense you get an inside view of problems from citizens. That is the real benefit. An under-standing of the department is acquired by these volunteers, and having them in the organization tends to ensure that the members of the regular organization are going to behave themselves in such a fashion as to withstand close public scrutiny. The least important benefit, but the most attractive, is community policing with no direct cost to the taxpayer.

In addition to these "official" volunteer programs, my department has businessmen's booster groups in each of our

17 geographic divisions. A booster group is composed of businessmen who may or may not reside in the community, but who have their businesses there. They want to help their police department and the community. For example, the police department might need a bus in a particular section of the community to get the kids to some youth activity. Some of our business groups have raised money and purchased a bus. Some of them have provided bats and balls and athletic trophies for police-related athletic events. Some have purchased skivvy shirts with the name of the supporting police division on them, as well as the name of the booster group. We have little black kids running around our city wearing Newton Street Booster Association T-shirts. Instead of identifying with gangsters or hoodlums, they are identifying with the police. Psychologically, this has a very beneficial effect on all the other black kids in an area where there had been a great estrangement from the police. Here you have little kids proudly wearing some kind of a police skivvy shirt. Just think of that! The cost of that shirt is probably less than a couple of dollars, but the value that kid has placed on it could not be bought.

On our Mexican-American east side, in the Hollenbeck area, I recently attended the dedication ceremonies for the Hollenbeck Businessmen's Police Association Athletic Center. They have built a gym because the Mexican kids in that area had no place to go, and, among other things, boxing has a great attraction to them. The Hollenbeck group, which has done this fantastic thing to bring these kids together with the police, contains not only some prosperous Mexican-Americans who do business in that community, but also WASP and Jewish businessmen, since this was once partially a Jewish community. Together they are doing a tremendous job for these kids. There is no cost to the police department or to the taxpayers. The city is going to get, in effect, the use of a building that will be privately owned, privately operated, without any expense or bother to the city. The cost of this structure is perhaps a third of a million dollars, and the city is getting it for nothing. Similar groups are working throughout Los Angeles.

We also have female groups who actively support the Basic-Car Plan and team policing. They organized themselves so that they could help send out meeting notices and make coffee and serve cookies. Some of their names are the Seventy-Seventh Street Dames, the Devonshire Dames, the Harbor Lites, the West Valley Blue Belles, and the North Hollywood Gals. These good women get together on occasion and have an open house for all the policemen in a particular area. And the women from all over the city show up and serve lunch to policemen on a lawn in front of a city building. At Christmas, for example, these wonderful ladies get together and serve, with a great deal of love and cheer, the best Christmas meal available anywhere in the city.

Groups like this bring black women, white women, Mexican-American women, and Asian women together, all working toward a common purpose for their police department. The fact that they serve a free meal is not the clincher; after all, most policemen would rather go out and get their own meal at their favorite eating spot than eat a picnic lunch on the lawn. But the important thing is that the people are dedicating themselves to making our city a safer city, and our policemen appreciate that effort.

As I have already mentioned, we also have police/clergy councils. Too much cannot be said about the importance of getting the clergy involved in the problem of crime in America. If they could be entirely successful at their job, we would not have a serious crime problem. I keep telling the clergymen, "You are the ones who are supposed to somehow or another get out and preach the word of God to these boys and girls. These kids will soon be mothers and fathers themselves. If these kids ran their lives on the basis of good religious principles, we would need fewer judges and fewer policemen."

There are a few other groups that we have to get together with and work with for the common purpose of preventing crime. The schools, for example, provide the opportunity for another type of program. There is fear in American schools today. Teachers are just waiting to work something out with policemen and administrators in education. Our school programs generally involve the junior and secondary education levels of teachers and administrators. They meet with police officers frequently and routinely so that common problems can be discussed. Believe me, those teachers need help. And policemen need the help of those teachers. They can do a tremendous amount for the police. They facilitate the ability of our policemen to go onto school campuses, just as the police attempt to facilitate the ability of teachers to instruct in a peaceful atmosphere.

We also have a Deputy Auxiliary Police program, which was created years ago, then eliminated for about 20 years, and has now been revitalized. The DAP idea was always one of the greatest things that we have ever had. It gets kids from about 9 up through 13 or 14 involved in legitimate work and recreation; mainly, it provides identification with the police. Instead of having a policeman run the DAP program, we have civilian leaders do it. This is the principle of leverage, getting the work done through other people.

Police/citizen involvement through organizations goes beyond just one person saying, "We are going to meet and work on a particular problem." It is accomplished in a fairly informal sort of way, because we recognize that formal structures tend to perpetuate themselves even when there is no need for their existence. The most important product of these groups is people working on the problem of crime in their community. The more people that are actively involved in the battle, the better our chances will be to win the war against crime.

I mentioned previously that I thought the most important thing a leader could leave behind him was a philosophy for his organization. Deeds and action are a necessary part of life, but it is a philosophy that gives substance to the deeds.

Much of what I have described in these pages has been a fulfillment of that philosophy throughout my career. With some luck, a small amount of that philosophy, the part that is good, will survive me and provide some guidance for my organization in the coming years. I hope society will be better for it. With the help of God and some good leaders, America will be a better place for future generations. The pervasive fear of crime will be a thing of the past. We will be stronger as a nation and our people will be happier, holding their heads high and blazing new trails for the cause of freedom.

Index

239

243

244